# Iran Air

## Flying the Homa



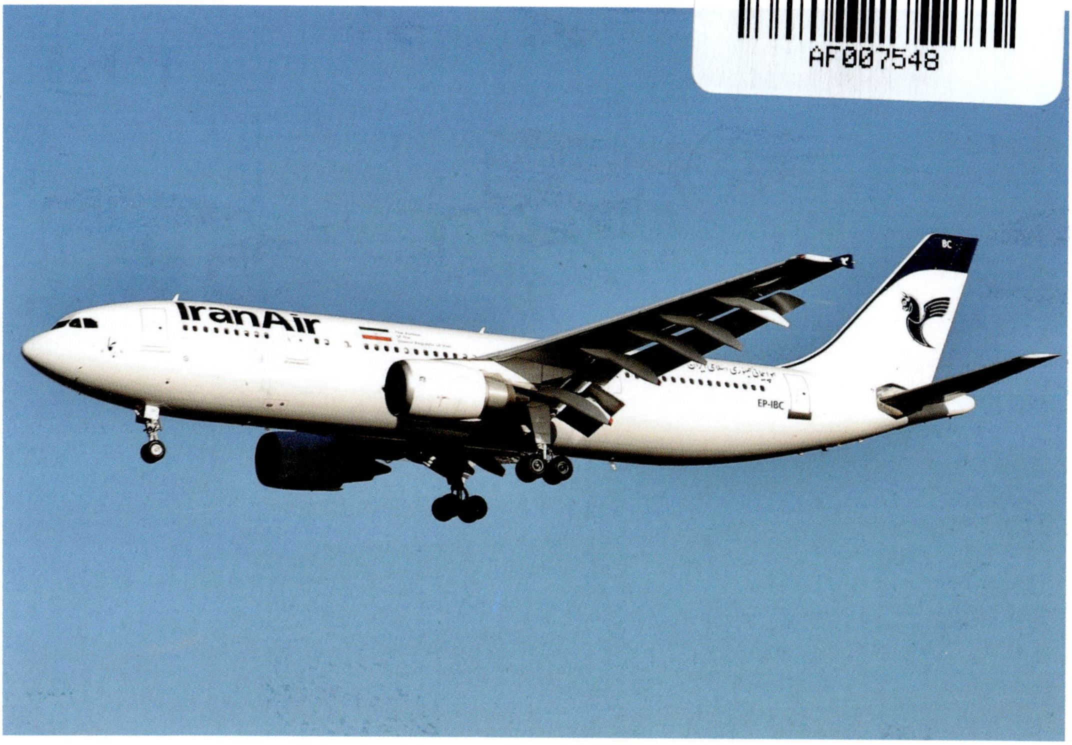

JOZEF MOLS

KEY Books

AIRLINES SERIES, VOLUME 9

**Front cover image**: Iran Air uses this Airbus A330 to compete with Mahan Air on long-haul flights. (Dara Zarbaf)

**Back cover image**: With new ATR equipment, Iran Air could start up both domestic and regional services. (Dara Zarbaf)

**Title page image**: The Airbus A300 was for a long time the backbone of the Iran Air fleet. (Alan Bushell)

**Contents page image**: This Airbus A321-200; built for Avianca, was delivered to Iran Air in 2017. (Dara Zarbaf)

Published by Key Books
An imprint of Key Publishing Ltd
PO Box 100
Stamford
Lincs PE19 1XQ

www.keypublishing.com

The right of Jozef Mols to be identified as the author of this book has been asserted in accordance with the Copyright, Designs and Patents Act 1988 Sections 77 and 78.

Copyright © Jozef Mols, 2022

ISBN 978 1 80282 264 9

All rights reserved. Reproduction in whole or in part in any form whatsoever or by any means is strictly prohibited without the prior permission of the Publisher.

Typeset by SJmagic DESIGN SERVICES, India.

# Contents

**Introduction and Acknowledgements** ..................................................................... 4
**Chapter 1**    Background ................................................................................................. 6
**Chapter 2**    First Passenger Flights ................................................................................ 8
**Chapter 3**    Iranian Airways .......................................................................................... 16
**Chapter 4**    The Creation of Iran Air ............................................................................. 24
**Chapter 5**    The Revolution ........................................................................................... 34
**Chapter 6**    Creativity and Self-sufficiency .................................................................. 45
**Chapter 7**    Improved Relations .................................................................................... 52
**Chapter 8**    The American Connection ........................................................................ 59
**Chapter 9**    The Consequences ..................................................................................... 66
**Chapter 10**   Covid-19 ..................................................................................................... 69
**Chapter 11**   The Outlook for Iran Air ............................................................................ 72
**Appendix 1**   Incidents and Accidents ............................................................................ 84
**Appendix 2**   Iran Air Fleet Details .................................................................................. 90
**Appendix 3**   Notes and References ............................................................................... 92

# Introduction and Acknowledgements

Persia – or Iran as it became known in 1935 – was once home to one of the world's oldest civilisations. It was one of the largest empires in history and can be described as the world's first superpower. Its influence reached not only all over Central Asia but also expanded across most of the Middle East and parts of Europe. However, even superpowers experience periods of growth and periods of decline. Invasions by Ottoman and Russian armies put an end to Persia's superpower status. Later on, in the early 20th century, Persia became the victim of the Great Game, a struggle for power between Russia and the United Kingdom, resulting in intrigue and occupation. In order to increase their influence, Russia and Great Britain, but also Germany and France, would supply Persia with its first aircraft. Switzerland also entered the scene by sending a young pilot by the name of Walter Mittelholzer to Persia to explore the possibility of setting up regular commercial services between Europe and Persia. But it would be a German aviation pioneer – Hugo Junkers – who would set up the first commercial airline in 1926.

The first truly Iranian airline was established after the end of World War Two by private investors. Later, some more small companies were set up until, in 1963, the Iranian government decided to take over and merge all existing private airlines, creating the Iran National Airline Corporation (later Iran Air). Under the rule of the Shah of Iran, Iran Air managed to expand and become one of the leading airlines in the Middle East. At one time, the airline even ordered Concordes. However, the Islamic Revolution in 1979 brought this expansion to an end, as foreign travellers had become worried about their safety when visiting the ancient empire in Central Asia.

Nevertheless, Iran Air continued its operations until international restrictions, followed by a boycott, made it impossible for the airline to obtain new aircraft or even spare parts for its existing fleet. The carrier only survived thanks to creativity and self-sufficiency. Under US President Barack Obama, agreements were signed between Iran and the West, limiting Iran's nuclear ambitions. Immediately afterwards, Iran Air placed mega-orders for aircraft with Boeing, Airbus and ATR. However, when President Donald Trump was inaugurated, the United States left the nuclear deal after only a handful of European aircraft had been delivered to Iran Air. European manufacturers were no longer able to deliver ordered aircraft, as the United States refused to issue export authorisations for aircraft that included more than 10 per cent of American-made parts.

Despite having only a few new aircraft and a limited supply of spare parts, Iran Air managed to continue its operations until Covid-19 hit the global airline industry. It is difficult to predict the future of the flag carrier. It is clear, however, that the results of new talks between the United States and Iran, started under President Biden, will be of the utmost importance.

I had the pleasure to fly aboard Iran Air's 737s for the first time in 1972 and later, when I lived in the Middle East, I was often a passenger aboard the airline's aircraft. As a former resident of the Gulf region, I continued to follow up on the fascinating evolution of aviation in that part of the world. It is my pleasure to share my experiences with the readers of this book. I wish to thank all the photographers who were so kind in making their pictures available for this publication. I also wish to express my gratitude to my partner, Marianne Van Leuvenhaege, for supporting me while writing this book and for being my first critical proofreader. Of course, my gratitude also goes to Key for publishing and distributing this book.

Jozef Mols<br>
Wommelgem (Belgium)<br>
15 May 2022

The Homa, which inspired the Iran Air logo. (Bernard Gagnon, CC BY-SA 4.0, https://creativecommons.org/licenses/by-sa/4.0, via Wikimedia Commons)

# Chapter 1
# **Background**

The history of an airline is so much more than just the story of pilots and planes. People and aircraft may seem the protagonists of this story, but they play their roles on a stage that is influenced, if not determined, by social and political events, geographic factors and religious evolutions. This is the case for all airlines around the world and maybe to an even larger extent for Iran Air. Therefore, a little knowledge of Iranian history is necessary to fully understand the background behind the country's flag carrier.

Of course, a full exploration of Iranian history would be far too extensive for this book. But we may remember from our schoolbooks that Iran is home to one of the world's oldest civilisations. Actually, excavations in northern Iran confirm a human presence in the country since the Lower Palaeolithic period. From the 10th to the 7th millennium BCE, early agricultural communities began to flourish.

The country was first unified by the Iranian Medes in the 7th century BCE and reached its territorial height in the 6th century BCE when Cyrus the Great founded the Achaemenid Empire. This would become one of the largest empires in history and has been described as the world's first superpower. Conquests under Cyrus and his successors expanded the empire to include Lydia (a region in Turkey), Babylon, Egypt, parts of the Balkans and Eastern Europe, as well as the lands to the west of the Indus and Oxus rivers. Also Azerbaijan, Armenia, Georgia, Anatolia in Turkey, Iraq, Syria, Lebanon, Jordan, Israel, Kuwait, northern Saudi Arabia, parts of the United Arab Emirates, Oman, Pakistan and Afghanistan had become part of the empire.

However, in 334 BCE, Alexander the Great invaded the Achaemenid Empire, defeating the last Achaemenid emperor, Darius III. Following the premature death of Alexander, the empire came under the control of the Hellenistic Seleucids. By the middle of the 2nd century BCE, the Parthian Empire rose to become the main power, and a century-long rivalry between the Romans and the Parthians began. The Parthian Empire would continue as a feudal monarchy for nearly five centuries before it was succeeded by the Sasanian Empire. Together with the neighbouring Byzantine (Eastern Roman) Empire, it made up the world's two most dominant powers for over four centuries.[1] Most of the history of the Sasanian Empire is, however, overshadowed by the Roman–Persian wars, which raged on the western borders of Anatolia, the Western Caucasus, Mesopotamia and the Levant for over 700 years. But these wars opened the way for an Arab invasion of Iran in the 7th century. A gradual process of state-imposed Islamization followed, including religious persecution of the Zoroastrian majority of Iran, demolition of libraries and burning of temples. In AD 750, the Abbasids overthrew the Umayyad Caliphate. Persians and Turks began to replace the Arabs in many fields, such as government, trade, and administration. After two centuries of Arab rule, semi-independent Iranian kingdoms began to appear on the fringes of the declining Abbasid Caliphate. The cultural revival, which began in the Abbasid period, led to the resurfacing of the Iranian national identity. Literature, philosophy, mathematics, medicine, astronomy and art blossomed again during a period known as the Islamic Golden Age. During this period, the first mythical stories in relation to aviation, and more specifically to the flight of kings and heroes, were depicted in poetry in the famous book of *Shahnameh* (The Epic of Kings: Hero Tales of Ancient Persia) created by the Persian poet Hakim Abol-Ghasem Ferdosi Toosi. Several references have been made in *Shahnameh*, eagles and demons or 'deev's', which have flown the Iranian kings and heroes. The most popular myths are about the flights of two kings, Kaikvoos and

Jamshid, and the Iranian hero Rostam. Mythologies aside, it is thought that some other experiments in relation to human flights may have been attempted throughout ancient Persia, which have, however, never been recorded.[2]

The 10th century saw a mass migration of Turkic tribes from Central Asia to the Iranian Plateau. Tribesmen were first used in the Abbasid Army as Mamluks (slave warriors). As a result, the mamluks would gain significant political power. In AD 999, large portions of Iran even came under the rule of Mamluks of Turkish origin. From 1219 to 1221, Iran suffered a devastating invasion by the Mongol Empire of Genghis Khan. According to some historians, Mongol violence killed three-quarters of the local population. In 1370, another conqueror by the name of Timur established the Timurid Empire, which lasted for another 156 years. The Timurids soon adopted the ways and customs of the Iranians and surrounded themselves with a culture that was distinctly Iranian.[3]

By 1500, Ismail I of Ardabil established the Safavid Empire. Beginning with Azerbaijan, he subsequently extended his authority over all of Greater Iran. Although, at that time, Iran was predominantly Sunni, Ismail instigated a forced conversion to the Shia branch of Islam. As a result, modern-day Iran is the only official Shia nation of the world. The Safavid era peaked under the reign of Abbas I, surpassing the Turkish arch-rivals in strength and making Iran a leading science and art hub in western Eurasia. The era also saw the start of mass integration from Caucasian populations into new layers of society in Iran, as well as mass resettlement of them within the heartlands of the country. Continuous wars with the Ottomans and Russian interference saw an end to the Safavid rule. In 1729, Nader Shah – a military genius from Khorasan – took back the annexed Caucasian territories that had been divided among the Ottoman and Russian authorities. He also invaded India but was later assassinated, which sparked a period of civil war and turmoil, bringing Karim Khan of the Zand dynasty to power. Upon his death, Agha Mohammad Khan came to power, establishing the Qajar dynasty in 1794. Following the disobedience of the Georgian subjects and their alliance with the Russians, the Qajars captured Tbilisi and drove the Russians out of the entire Caucasus, re-establishing Iranian suzerainty over the region.[4] Subsequent Russo-Iranian wars resulted in large territorial losses for Iran in the Caucasus, including the loss of Georgia, Armenia and Azerbaijan.

Between 1872 and 1905, a series of protests took place in response to the sale of concessions to foreigners by Qajar monarchs, which led to the Constitutional Revolution in 1905. The first Iranian constitution and the first national parliament of Iran were founded in 1906 through the ongoing revolution. Under the pretext of restoring order, the Russians occupied northern Iran in 1911 and maintained a military presence in the region for years to come. This Russian occupation should be seen in the light of the 'Great Game': a confrontation between British and Russian power in Central Asia. Although the epicentre of this confrontation was located in neighbouring Afghanistan, both powers also tried to establish their influence in Iran. Although Iran remained neutral during World War One, Ottoman, Russian and British troops would occupy the territory of western Iran and fought the Persian campaign before fully withdrawing their forces in 1921. The inability of the Qajar government to maintain the country's sovereignty during and immediately after World War One led to the British-directed Persian coup d'état and Reza Shah's establishment of the Pahlavi dynasty. Reza Shah became the new prime minister of Iran and was declared the new monarch in 1925.

It was during this period following the Constitutional Revolution that Iranians would, for the first time, see an aeroplane flying over Tehran. The aircraft landed at a place known then as Meidan Mashgh – an army exercise field in the city centre. The aircraft was a Blériot XI flown into Tehran from Russia by a Russian pilot. After some repair work at the army repair shop, the aircraft was flown back to Russia.[5]

# Chapter 2
# First Passenger Flights

A country's aviation history often reveals that its air force has played an important role in the early formation of commercial air transportation in the country. This was certainly the case in Iran. As a matter of fact, the first Iranian passengers were flown in Iranian Air Force aircraft. The air force also carried mail, small packages and, occasionally, civilian passengers.

Before World War One, there was no reason for Iran to set up its own air force. In 1921, however, when the historical coup d'état ended the Qajar dynasty, the supreme commander of the armed forces, Reza Khan, contemplated the foundation of an Iranian Air Force. Due to the situation in the country in the early 1920s, military aeroplanes were deemed highly valuable for chasing the mutinous groups in different parts of the country.[1] The mission of obtaining aircraft for the air force started in 1922, when the Iranian ambassador in Washington, DC requested to purchase aircraft from the United States, as well as assistance for the training of pilots and technicians. However, the request was denied due to American commitments to the disarmament treaty of World War One. So, Iran had to turn to European countries such as Germany, Russia and France. The story about the introduction of European aircraft is a little bit ambiguous. But it is certain that a German-made Junkers F 13 was purchased and brought to Iran. Since there were no provisions in the budget for the purchase of more aircraft, the Iranian prime minister asked the Iranian people to raise funds to order these aircraft. Following this request, the populations of the Gilan and Mazanderan provinces raised enough funds to purchase two more Junkers F 13s.

Informed about the German–Iranian deal, Russia agreed to sell aircraft to Iran as well. At that time, de Havilland DH-4 and DH-9 aircraft were built in Russia where they were called R-1 and R-5. An Avro 504 was also obtained via Russia. These aircraft were delivered in 1923. Finally, France, too, agreed to sell some aircraft to Iran. This deal included delivery of Spad-42, Potez-8, Breguet-14 and Breguet-19 aircraft from France. As a result of these purchases, Iran decided its pilots should be trained in France and the Soviet Union. In June 1923, the first group of officers was dispatched to France for training. After completing his instruction in February 1925, Colonel Ahmad Khan Jakjavan left Paris on a Breguet 19, which was marked with an Iranian flag and logo, to land on the Gala Morgi airfield. He was the first Iranian pilot and would later become the commander-in-chief of the Iranian Air Force. In June 1924, ten more officers were sent to the Soviet Union for flight training. They were later commissioned to fly three newly purchased de Havilland DH-9As to Iran (but if rumours are correct, only one aircraft would reach Tehran). Germany contributed to the training of Iranian pilots by sending a single instructor by the name of Schefer to Iran. At that time, the Iranian Air Force had a total of 33 aircraft of nine different models. They were mainly used for pilot training but, once in a while, also transported limited numbers of passengers and small amounts of mail.

Around the same time, a young Swiss pilot and aerial photographer by the name of Walter Mittelholzer arrived in Iran. He had completed his instruction as a military pilot in Switzerland in 1918 and had subsequently set up a small airline by the name of Comte, which was later renamed Ad Astra Aero (and went on to become Swissair). On 18 December 1924, the young pilot made his first transcontinental long-distance flight, which amounted to 71 hours of flying time from Zürich to Bushir on the Persian Gulf. He continued his flight to Tehran and returned home with magnificent aerial pictures of Iran. The aircraft was sold to the government and remained in Iran. On this flight,

Mittelholzer used a Junkers A 20 aircraft with a 250hp BMW engine. Unsurprisingly, the arrival of this plane increased Iranian interest in German-made aircraft.[2]

The Junkers company had been established in Germany in 1895 and was originally a manufacturer of thermodynamic products. But Hugo Junkers was also one of the most prominent German aviation pioneers. In February 1922, Junkers signed an agreement with Russia to erect an aircraft factory there where he started assembling aircraft. The peace treaty that followed World War One made it difficult for German aircraft manufacturers to fully develop their industry, so Junkers decided to continue his activities outside the country. After the set-up of the factory in Russia, Junkers incorporated the Junkers Luftverkehr Russia airline, which performed domestic services in the Soviet Union. But when, by 1924, the Soviets set up their own airline, Junkers airline's activities in that country discontinued and its attention was focused on Persia.

In September 1924, Junkers contacted the Persian government with a proposal to operate postal services between Baku and Bandar Pahlavi (today Bandar Anzali), as well as a Stockholm–Moscow–Tehran service. While the government was studying his proposals, Junkers started some non-scheduled flights between Baku and Tehran. The first of these flights took place on 21 December 1924 and the flights would continue until March 1925, when they were suspended because Persia did not pay the promised subventions. In the meantime, Imperial Airways wanted to open an air service between Cairo and Karachi along the Persian coast. The French CIDNA (Compagnie International de Navigation Aérienne) airline also showed interest in operations in Persia. But it was clear the Shah had no intention of allowing British or French airlines to operate in his country.

In 1926 – as a result of his proposals – Junkers could sign a five-year agreement with the government to set up an airline and perform domestic flights within Persia. At the same time, Junkers was asked to set up a training school for pilots and technicians. The new airline was called Junkers Luftverkehr Persia and it established its main base at Doushan Tappeh. Junkers decided to use a fleet of Junkers F 13 aircraft, each capable of carrying two pilots and four passengers. These aircraft had previously been based in Moscow and were transferred to the new airline shortly after the signing of the agreement.[3] The first routes were from Tehran to Bandar Pahlavi in the north and from Tehran to Ghasr Shirin via Hamedan and Kermanshah in the west. One should keep in mind that, at the time Junkers started his operations, regular passenger flights were still a novelty and Iran was even still building railroads.[4] An international route to Moscow was opened in co-operation with Ukrainian airline company Ukrvozdukhput. Junkers Luftverkehr guaranteed the Tehran–Bandar Pahlavi leg of the flight, and Ukrvozdukhput was in charge of the continuation of the flight to Moscow. A little bit later, a third domestic route from Tehran to Mashad was opened.

In April and June 1927, two new Junkers F 13s arrived from Germany and, in August, the first Junkers W.33 was added to the fleet, followed by a Junkers G 31, which arrived in September. As a cholera epidemic was spreading across the south of Persia, the government asked for assistance from the airline. Physicians and treatment serum were transported to different locations in the southern part of the country. During these operations, the G 31 crashed with 20 passengers on board. Nobody was hurt and the aircraft was repaired and sent back to Germany.

In April 1928, a new route from Tehran via Esfahan and Shiraz to Bushehr was added to the network. When the original five-year contract between Junkers and the government neared its end, Junkers proposed the setting up of a military flying school in Persia. But, as the original agreement stipulated that Junkers had to train two pilots and two technicians every year – something he never did – the government took its time to renew the permission to fly domestic services. Hoping the agreement would be extended anyhow, the Junkers airline started up a service linking Tehran and Baghdad. However, only a few months later, the route was discontinued as it became clear the licence to operate in Persia would not be extended for another period. As a result, in October 1931, the airline started to close down and began reducing its services. In the meantime, the Anglo Persian Oil Company (APOC) had chartered one F 13 from Junkers to transport 'technicians and equipment', but it was soon discovered that the airline was mainly transporting … opium.[5] After Junkers closed down its operations, the APOC plane remained in Persia until the end of 1931. Other aircraft of the Junkers fleet remained idle on the aerodrome, finally being returned to Germany in September 1933.

When Junkers left Persia in 1932, there were no commercial air services left in the country. Therefore, the air force occasionally provided postal services and randomly transported some civilian passengers, particularly government officials and employees.

*Above*: The family of Mostofi-Al-Mamlik (Prime Minister during the Qajar and Pahlavi eras) with Qajar women in front of an imported aeroplane at Qala-i-Marghi Airport. (Institute of Contemporary Iranian History Studies, Harvard University, public domain)

*Left*: A Qajar girl with two foreign pilots in front of an imported aircraft at Qala-i-Marghi Airport. (Harvard Library of Middle Eastern Studies, public domain)

A Junkers F 13 of the Junkers Luftverkehr Persien in Tehran. (Deutsches Museum München, public domain)

Walter Mittelholzer's Junkers in Bushir in 1925. (ETH-Bibliothek Zürich, Bildarchiv/Stiftung Luftbild Schweiz/ Fotograf: Mittelholzer, Walter/LBS_MH02-02-0207-AL-FL/Public Domain Mark)

**Walter Mittelholzer's arrival in Isfahan. (ETH-Bibliothek Zürich, Bildarchiv/Stiftung Luftbild Schweiz/Fotograf: Unknown/LBS_MH02-02-0230-AL-FL/Public Domain Mark)**

**A Junkers aircraft in Isfahan in 1925. (ETH-Bibliothek Zürich, Bildarchiv/Stiftung Luftbild Schweiz/Fotograf: Unknown/LBS_MH02-02-0157-AL-FL/Public Domain Mark)**

**Arrival of the first Junkers F 13 of Junkers Luftverkehr Persien in Tehran, in 1923. (ETH Bibliothek Zürich, public domain)**

**Junkers presented his aircraft during an aviation day in Tehran. (ETH Bibliothek Zürich, public domain)**

This Junkers F 13 was imported from Russia and was used by Junkers Luftverkehr Persien. The aircraft is seen here over Tehran. (ETH-Bibliothek Zürich, Bildarchiv/Stiftung Luftbild Schweiz/Fotograf: Mittelholzer, Walter/LBS_MH02-02-0089-AL-FL/Public Domain Mark)

A Junkers F 13 of Junkers Luftverkehr Persien flying over Tehran. (ETH-Bibliothek Zürich, Bildarchiv/Stiftung Luftbild Schweiz/Fotograf: Mittelholzer, Walter/LBS_MH02-02-0090-AL-FL/Public Domain Mark)

An airmail letter, inaugurating the mail service from Tehran via Isfahan and Shiraz to Bushir. (Jozef Mols collection)

Anglo Persian Oil Company (APOC) chartered aircraft from Junkers Luftverkehr Persien to fly staff and equipment to the oil fields. (APOC, public domain)

# Chapter 3
# Iranian Airways

When, in 1932, the Junkers airline ceased operations, the Ministry of Post and Telegraph took over the responsibility to deliver air mail. But in the early years, it was the air force that performed the flights. In 1938, the Iranian government decided to set up an airline for the ministry under the name of Iranian State Airlines. For that purpose, Iran bought two British de Havilland DH 89 Dragon Rapides. Later, two more aircraft of the same type joined the fleet. Two air force pilots were sent to England to be trained on these aircraft. The planes were shipped via Khoramshahr to Tehran. After their assembly, they were used on services between Tehran and Baghdad. Scheduled services started on 15 March 1938 and operated once a week on the Tehran–Kermanshah–Baghdad route. This flight, executed by Iranian pilots, took about five hours one way. Later, another service between Tehran, Isfahan, Shiraz and Bushir was added. (It was the intention to also set up co-operation with Turkish Airlines on flights connecting Tehran with Istanbul, but this connection remained unfulfilled until the end of World War Two.[1]) The airline also carried passengers on these flights. Imperial Airways provided some assistance for these operations. Iranian State Airlines would continue to fly these services during World War Two until 1946.[2] One of the Dragon Rapides crashed in 1939 and the ordered replacement never arrived.[3]

Obviously, the outbreak of World War Two would seriously affect air transportation in Iran. Traditional Iranian dislike of Great Britain made any political alliance with that country impossible. Germany, on the other hand, had increased its influence in Iran, but this country was also viewed with suspicion, although it was mainly German technicians who kept Iranian planes flying by providing technical assistance. For Iran, neutrality was the only acceptable policy, which was, in fact, encouraged by Germany. When German troops advanced through the southern parts of the Soviet Union against the Caucasus, the Allies considered the strong German presence in Iran unacceptable. On 17 August 1941, the Soviet Union and Great Britain demanded the expulsion of German personnel working in Iran. The Iranian government rejected this demand and, as a consequence, British and Soviet troops launched a surprise invasion on 25 August 1941[4]; the Reza Shah's government quickly surrendered. The invasion's strategic purpose was to secure a supply line to the Soviet Union (later named the Persian Corridor) in such a way that the United States could ship war supplies to the Soviet troops via Iran under the Lend-Lease agreement between both countries. For that purpose, an American aircraft assembly plant was set up in Abadan. Another purpose of the invasion was to secure the oil fields and the Abadan Refinery of the AIOC. Furthermore, the Allies wanted to prevent a German advance via Turkey on Baku's oil fields and limit German influence in Iran. On 16 September 1941, following the invasion, Reza Shah abdicated and was replaced by Mohammad Reza Pahlavi, his 21-year-old son.[5]

All civil flying in Iran was strictly controlled after 1941 and the three Dragon Rapides of Iranian State Airlines were allocated serial numbers HK 915, HK 916 and HK 917. In August 1944, three ex-RAF DH 89 Dominies were delivered to Iran. They were all eventually added to the diminutive fleet of the State Airlines, which was reconstructed as the Skerkat Shami Havapeimace Iran.[6]

In the meantime, during the Tehran Conference in 1943, the Allied 'Big Three' – Joseph Stalin, Franklin D. Roosevelt and Winston Churchill – signed the Tehran Declaration to guarantee the post-war independence and boundaries of Iran. However, at the end of the war, Soviet troops remained in Iran and established two puppet states in north-western Iran, namely the People's Government of Azerbaijan and the Republic of Mahabad. This led to the Iran crisis of 1946 – one of the first confrontations of the Cold War – which ended after oil concessions were promised to the Soviet Union and Soviet forces withdrew from Iran in May 1946.

Notwithstanding the war, young people were dreaming of setting up a new private airline in the post-war period. In December 1944, a group of influential and affluent Iranian investors formed Iranian Airways as a private airline. Some of these investors also set up Irantour, the first Iranian travel and tour organisation. Gholam Hossein Ebtehaj would become the first managing director of Iranian Airways and Irantour. Simultaneously with the formation of Iranian Airways, an agreement for technical assistance was signed with Trans World Airlines (TWA). In turn, TWA bought a 10 per cent share in the new airline. By the end of March 1945, the airline managed to buy three surplus American C-47s. As these aircraft could be bought at cheap prices following the war, the airline continued to buy such planes each time the occasion presented itself. At one point, the total number of C-47s stood at 20. At first, most pilots and technical personnel were American. However, by the end of 1946, the first three pilots (Colonel Mostafavai, Major Khademi and Captain Rafat) were assigned from the Iranian Air Force to fly with Iranian Airways. The first scheduled flights started from Tehran to the Holy City of Mashad, followed by Tehran-Isfahan-Shiraz flights which, after an overnight stop, continued to Bushir, Abadan and Ahwaz. A limited number of flights to Zahedan were also offered. One has to note that, following World War Two, none of the Iranian airports was fully operational. Therefore, operations largely depended upon improvisation by the crews.

In the summer of 1946, the airline started up its first international services. Baghdad, Beirut and Cairo became its first destinations, followed by Tel Aviv. Immigration to Israel was growing, so the decision to include this country on the route map was logical. Later on, the flight to Beirut was expanded into a Beirut–Athens–Paris service. For that occasion, Iranian Airways opened an office in the French capital. It was a big surprise to learn that G H Ebtehaj, one of the airline's founders, appointed a young man by the name of Houshang Tajadod as the second-in-command of Iranian Airways. He would later become an icon of the Iranian airline industry and a key member within the top management of the later Iran Air. Another remarkable decision (for a Muslim country) was the hiring of a female pilot. Ina Avshid, who had obtained her pilot's licence from the Civil Aviation Club, became one of the company's Douglas DC-3 pilots and the first female pilot of an Iranian passenger aircraft.

When the co-operation agreement with TWA expired, the French company Cie Générale de Transport (CGT) became involved and provided technical assistance. In 1949, Reza Afshar took over 70 per cent of the Iranian Airways shares and assumed the responsibilities of managing director. One of his first decisions was to cancel the contract with the French CGT. In 1953, CGT was replaced by Trans Ocean Airlines from the United States which provided assistance in a variety of domains such as operations, maintenance, sales and administration. Furthermore, the American airline also supplied two Convair aircraft under a lease agreement. Besides the Convairs and the C-47s, Iranian Airways also used some Skymasters, DC-4s and DC-6s.

By now, the political scene in Iran had changed. In 1951, Mohammad Mosaddegh was appointed as prime minister. He became very popular in the country after he nationalised Iran's petroleum industry and oil reserves – a decision he would soon regret. In 1953, an Anglo-American covert operation was set up to depose Mosaddegh. After the departure of his prime minister, the Shah of Iran became increasingly autocratic and Iran entered a decade-long phase of controversially close relations with the United States.[7]

In 1958, the Iranian government bought three Vickers Viscounts which, at that time, were considered luxury planes. The aircraft were put at the disposal of Iranian Airways. They came at the right time as the airline had expanded its route map to include 14 domestic and ten regional destinations, including Afghanistan, Pakistan, India, Iraq, Saudi Arabia, Syria, Lebanon, Dubai and Kuwait. Cargo-only operations had been started up to Ankara, Milan, Zürich and Frankfurt. Although the airline was expanding, it could not grow swiftly enough to reach the ideal level needed to meet the demand and expectations of the Iranian people, mainly due to limited financial resources. Furthermore, a series of four crashes had jeopardised the company's reputation.

Besides Iranian Airways, another private airline had been set up in 1954 by Ahmad Shafigh (son of the Shah's twin sister). Persian Air Services (PAS) was intended to become a mainly cargo airline. The airline received technical support from the British company Skyways. PAS started operating cargo services from Tehran via Abadan to Beirut, Brindisi and Basle. It also operated a Tehran-Geneva flight, flown by an Avro York, which it chartered from Trans Mediterranean Airways of Lebanon. Later, Belgian carrier Sabena would lease a Douglas DC-7C aircraft to PAS, with which routes to Geneva, Paris, Brussels and London could be organised.

In August 1961, Iranian Airways and PAS decided to merge under the new brand name of United Iranian Airlines. Although this short-lived merger seemed to be more of a formality than a practical step, and nothing was actually changed in the day-to-day operations, the fleet livery illustrated the name of the new company.[8]

**After the departure of the Junkers Luftverkehr Persiens, military pilots took over the transportation of airmail. This picture shows the departure of the first flight from Tehran to Isfahan. (Jozef Mols collection, public domain)**

During the British and American occupation of Iran, the Allies used the country as a gateway to Russia to supply weapons via the Persian Corridor. This picture shows an assembly plant for American aircraft somewhere in Iran. (Library of Congress, public domain)

These American aircraft have been prepared at the Abadan Airport in Iran for delivery to Russia via the Persian Corridor. (National Museum of the US Air Force, public domain)

*Left*: An aircraft of the RAF's No. 237 Squadron at an Iranian base during World War Two. (Imperial War Museum, public domain)

*Below*: A group of Iranian pilots during their training. (Massoud Malek, CC BY-SA 4.0, via Wikimedia Commons)

Delivery of the first Douglas C-47 (DC-3 Dakota) to Iran. (Massoud Malek, CC BY-SA 4.0, via Wikimedia Commons)

An Iranian Airways Douglas DC-3. (Gerhard Haubold, Creative Commons Licence, via Wikimedia Commons)

Iranian Airways was the first private Iranian airline and used up to 20 Douglas DC-3 aircraft. (Eddie Coates collection)

This PAS timetable from 1961 shows the Douglas DC-7C obtained via Sabena. (David Zekria collection, timetableimages.com)

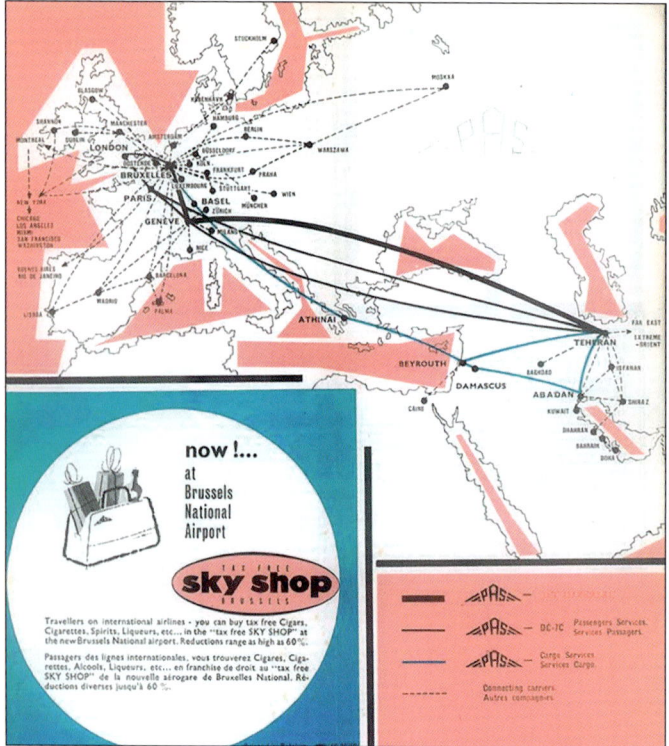

The PAS route map from the airline's 1961 timetable. (David Zekria collection, timetableimages.com)

*Right*: A PAS Douglas DC-7C at Tehran airport. (Unknown photographer, public domain, via Wikimedia Commons)

*Below*: A PAS Douglas DC-7C ready for departure. (Jozef Mols collection, public domain)

# Chapter 4
# The Creation of Iran Air

When PAS and Iranian Airways merged into United Iranian Airlines, the deal would last only for a very limited time. In February 1963, the Iranian parliament issued a decree to allow a new company – the Iran National Airline Corporation – to take over United Iranian Airlines. By acquiring all its assets, which were the combined resources of Iranian Airways and PAS, the new carrier started out with a very mixed fleet. Major General Ali Mohammad Khademi, until then the Iranian Air Force chief of staff, was appointed as the first manager of the national airline. He would remain in office for 17 years. For many of the airline's 700 workers, the creation of the national airline gave no reason for cheers or celebration. In their opinion, converting the carrier into a government entity would hinder its progress.

In 1964, Iran National Airline Corporation became a member of IATA. Obviously, the airline was in search of a logo. A competition was announced, judged by a group of members of the College of Fine Arts. A young Iranian by the name of Edward Zohrabian was proclaimed the winner with his griffin, inspired by a statue atop one of the columns at Persepolis. For practical reasons, the name 'Iran National Airline Corporation' would later be abbreviated to Iran Air (domestically, it was called the Homa, both in reference to the logo and because the acronym of the airline in Persian was 'HOMA'). Domestic flights were operated with the fleet of aircraft obtained from United Iranian Airlines, including Douglas DC-3s, Douglas DC-6s, Vickers Viscounts and some de Havilland Dragon Rapides that had survived World War Two. A number of Beechcraft Model 18 aircraft, which had served with PAS, were integrated into the Iran Air fleet alongside some Convair 240s. There are also rumours indicating the airline might have used a single Lockheed Constellation, but there is no evidence to substantiate this information. Our research only found an Iranian banknote, showing a drawing of the Constellation in Iran Air colours.

One of the airline's most important objectives was to modernise its fleet. During the early 1960s, no advanced airline could continue to operate with propeller aircraft, as the Jet Age had started. Of course, the introduction of jets would be a long and complicated process, including the choice of a manufacturer. The mixed equipment concept, i.e., buying from more than one manufacturer, was immediately eliminated as the operation of aircraft built by diverse manufacturers would have been a nightmare in terms of maintenance and supply. Following a market study, it was decided to obtain different aircraft in different sizes from Boeing, all powered by Pratt & Whitney engines. To test the concept, a single Boeing 727-100 was leased for a one-year period, during which time the aircraft was used on several routes, including to Istanbul, Rome, Geneva, Frankfurt, Paris, London, Karachi and Bombay (now Mumbai), as well as to several of the Gulf states. After this test period, an order was placed with Boeing for several aircraft models.

In 1965, Iran Air took delivery of its first jet aircraft. Boeing 707s and 727-100s arrived in Tehran, followed by Boeing 737-200s in 1971, a stretched Boeing 727-200 in 1974 and a series of Boeing 747 variants (747-100, 747-200 and 747 SP) between 1978 and 1979. Thanks to the introduction of these jets, Iran Air could serve most European cities with non-stop and one-stop flights, including over 30 flights to London alone. On 29 May 1971, a Tehran–New York route was inaugurated using the Boeing 707, which made a stopover at London Heathrow. In summer, however, these flights had to be discontinued because the high temperature in Tehran reduced the payload, meaning fewer passengers could be booked on the flights, making them uneconomical. But when the Boeing 747s arrived, the route was upgraded to a non-stop flight using the 747SP. With this flight, Iran Air set a new world record in time and distance for a non-stop scheduled long-haul flight (12 hours and 15 minutes, 6,131 miles).[1] At the same time, plans were made to start up flights from Tehran to Los Angeles, and Iran Air offices were opened in Los Angeles, Houston and Chicago.

In 1978, the airline acquired six Airbus A300 aircraft – leased from Airbus – for use on its domestic trunk and busy regional routes. By the end of that year, Iran Air was serving 31 international destinations, including New York, Beijing and Tokyo. Plans were made to offer direct services to Los Angeles and Sydney, for which the airline's Boeing 747SP would be ideal. In this way, Iran Air might have used Tehran as a hub for connections between the East and West. However, the dream was never fulfilled, although there is no doubt that, by the end of the 1970s, Iran Air was the fastest growing airline in the world and also one of the most profitable.[2] It carried around five million passengers per year.

Owing to the first oil crisis in 1973 and the spike in oil prices, the economy of Iran was flooded with foreign currency. For the Iranian government, the sky was the limit. In this context it is not surprising the Shah of Iran wanted to buy the most modern equipment for his national flag carrier. On 2 March 1969, the Aérospatiale Concorde had made its first flight and the Iranian head of state wanted to buy some of these aircraft for Iran Air to bolster its prestige. In June 1972, a Concorde was flown to Tehran while on a 30-day tour of the Middle East, Far East and Australia. The Iran Air experts studied the aircraft very closely and concluded (and rightly believed) that the aircraft, economically and operationally, was not the right choice for Iran Air. Furthermore, they were not very optimistic about the Concorde's future. But since the Shah had made the decision to order three Concordes on 8 October 1972, they now had to convince him that buying the aircraft was not a viable project for Iran Air. It seemed an impossible task to convince the Shah to abandon his dream. It would be Houshang Tajadod, Iran Air's first post-revolution managing director, who could cancel the order in February 1980 after Iran Air had briefly operated a chartered Concorde on flights between Tehran and Paris.

During the 1970s, Iran Air also decided to diversify its activities and get involved in other aviation-related businesses. Iran Airtour was established in 1973 by Iran Air. Its main task was to conduct domestic and international charter flights for groups as well as the organisation of travel tours. This way, the new subsidiary was supposed to contribute to the expansion of the tourism industry. At the beginning of its operation, Iran Airtour launched tours from Tehran to the holy city of Mashhad. Due to the success of cultural and pilgrimage tours, Iran Airtour extended the operation to include tours to Sharjah, Dubai, China, India, Kuala Lumpur and Singapore.

Homa Hotel Group – a subsidiary of Iran Air – acquired and managed a group of hotels in Tehran, Shiraz, Persepolis, Bandar Abbas, Ramsar and Mashhad. The construction of a new 42-storey hotel in Tehran was started, which would have become the tallest building in the entire Middle East. At the same time, Iran Air intended to buy a large hotel in London as well as the Intercontinental hotel chain owned by Pan American Airways. In charge of the hotel group was Jubin Shekoohian, an experienced hotelier and Iran Air's former catering director. Besides hotel accommodation, Iran Air also provided passenger, ramp and in-flight catering services to most airlines calling at Tehran Mehrabad Airport.

United Iranian Airlines was the result of the short-lived merger of PAS and Iranian Airways. (Jozef Mols collection, public domain)

When Iran National Airline Corporation was set up, the airline obtained the aircraft from both PAS and Iranian Airways, including this DC-3. (Ed Coates collection)

This Dakota entered the Iran National Airline Corporation's fleet after the government nationalised the airline industry. (Ed Coates collection)

Iran National Air Lines' Vickers Viscount. (Unknown photographer, via Wikimedia Commons Licence, public domain)

This Douglas DC-6B was also taken over by the Iran National Airline Corporation. (Jozef Mols collection)

A former PAS Douglas DC-6B in the livery of the Iran National Airline Corporation. (Jozef Mols collection)

An Iran National Airline Corporation Viscount at the Isfahan airport in 1962. (Verity Cridland, CC BY 2.0 https://creativecommons.org/licenses/by/2.0, via Wikimedia Commons)

After a while, the Iran National Airline Corporation title was changed to Iranair as seen on this Douglas DC-3. (Ed Coates collection)

Iran Air also used some de Havilland Dragon Rapides that had survived the war. (Alan Bushell collection)

An Iran Air de Havilland 89A Dominie in the maintenance hangar. (Alan Bushell collection)

The author found no proof that Iran Air used the Lockheed Constellation, but the Constellation is depicted on this Iranian banknote. (Jozef Mols collection)

## The Creation of Iran Air

*Above*: When Iran Air obtained its first jet aircraft, the Iran National Airlines Corporation title was still used, like on this Boeing 727-86, seen at Zürich Airport. (ETH-Bibliothek Zurich, Bildarchiv/Stiftung Luftbild Schweiz/Fotograf: Swissair/LBS_SR04-055421/ CC BY-SA 4.0)

*Right*: Iran Air timetable 1968–69. (Alan Buschell collection)

*Above*: The route map of the 1968–69 timetable. (Alan Buschell collection)

*Left*: This Fokker F28 Mark 1000 Fellowship was chartered in 1971 by Iran Air for the 2,500th anniversary of the Persian Empire. (Thijs Postma)

To meet growing demand, Iran Air had to lease several aircraft, like this Douglas DC-8, leased from Martinair in Holland. (Jozef Mols collection)

In 1956, the airline obtained this Convair CV-240 from Babb & Company. (Peter Keating via Alan Bushell Collection)

# Chapter 5
# The Revolution

By the end of the 1970s, Iran Air had become a well-respected, safe and fast-growing airline. However, the gigantic income generated from increasing oil prices had caused inflation. By 1974, the economy was experiencing double-digit inflation while, at the same time, corruption was rampant. By 1975 and 1976, an economic recession had led to increased unemployment, especially among the millions of youths who had migrated to the cities of Iran looking for construction jobs. Opposition against the Shah's regime was growing.[1] While, on the one hand, the Shah was trying to modernise the country at a very fast pace and citizens of larger cities understood and enjoyed this move, people in more rural areas – with less access to education and information – had a hard time adjusting to a modern Western-style society. They turned to religion in search of stability and peace of mind. The Islamic Revolution began in January 1978, with the first major demonstrations being held against the Shah. After a year of strikes and demonstrations paralysing the country's economy, Mohammad Reza Pahlavi fled Iran. Political and religious leader Ayatollah Ruhollah Khomeini, who had been exiled for his opposition to the Shah, returned from said exile in Paris on an Air France flight and formed a new government. After a referendum in April 1979, Iran officially became an Islamic republic. A second referendum in December of the same year approved a theocratic constitution. Just a few days after the revolution ended, Houshang Tajadod, a pioneer and the most qualified and senior manager of Iran Air, was appointed as managing director of Iran Air by Mehdi Bazargan, the country's first post-revolution prime minister. However, it wasn't long before Tajadod offered his resignation. Chasem Shakibnia, a former deputy minister of post, telephone and telegraph in the previous governments, succeeded him. Being a member of Prime Minister Bazargan's cabinet, he also resigned when Bazargan himself quit his post. Finally, Cyrus Chaichian, the deputy managing director for commercial affairs, was appointed managing director. But Chaichian also resigned after only four months on the job. Between 1979 and 2007, Iran Air would have ten managing directors, all from outside the company.

Just before the revolution, Iran Air's fleet of widebody and long-range aircraft included two Boeing 747-200s and three Boeing 747SP aircraft, used on flights from Tehran to New York. For international flights to East Asian and European destinations, as well as regional and domestic flights, the airline operated a fleet of nine Boeing 727s, four Boeing 737s and six Boeing 707s. Furthermore, six Airbus B3 aircraft were on order for delivery in 1981. In addition, three other Boeing 747-100s were ordered, but the occurrence of the revolution led to the cancellation of their purchase contract by the new managers of Iran Air. Two of the Boeing 747s, delivered after the revolution, were not even painted in Iran Air's colours and were grounded for sale at Mehrabad Airport due to the so-called luxury items on board the planes.

The new situation resulting from the revolution did not please every Iranian. A nationwide uprising against the new government began in 1979 with the Kurdish rebellion and the Khuzestan uprisings, along with a revolt in Baluchestan. Over the following years, these revolts would be subdued in a violent manner by the government. In the meantime, on 4 November 1979, a group of Muslim students seized the United States Embassy in Tehran and took 52 staff members hostage after the United States had refused to extradite Mohammad Reza Pahlavi to Iran. Despite attempts by President Jimmy Carter's administration to negotiate the release of the hostages, and a failed rescue attempt, the hostages were not liberated until the moment Ronald Reagan came to power in the United States. The Shah left the United States and was exiled to Egypt, where he died. The United States imposed several sanctions against Iran, which damaged the aspirations of its flag carrier, Iran Air. To make matters worse, on 22 September 1980, the Iraqi Army invaded the western Iranian province of Khuzestan, beginning the Iran–Iraq War.[2] Although Iraqi President Saddam Hussein's army made several early advances, by mid-1982 the Iranian forces had managed to drive the Iraqi Army back into Iraq. In July 1982, with the Iraqi forces thrown back on the defensive, the regime in Tehran decided to invade Iraq and several offensives were conducted in a bid to conquer Iraqi territory and capture cities, including Basra. The war would go on until 1988 when the Iraqi Army defeated the Iranian forces inside Iraq and pushed the remaining troops back across the border. Subsequently, Khomeini accepted a truce mediated by the United Nations. Following the end of the war in 1989, Akbar Hashemi Rafsanjani and his administration concentrated on a pragmatic pro-business policy trying to rebuild and strengthen the economy. It is clear that during the war, domestic and international travel were considerably reduced. This was in part due to the war and to almost full restrictions on Iranians travelling abroad.

Due to the revolution and the Iran–Iraq war, plus the subsequent series of sanctions, Iranian airlines were cut off from access to the outside world in terms of aircraft purchases. Throughout the 1980s, Iran's airline scene was limited to three major airlines: flag carrier Iran Air, its charter subsidiary Iran Airtour Airlines and Iran Aseman Airlines. However, the sanctions had little impact on the operation of the airlines at first. Iran Air continued to receive new Airbus A300s until January 1983, but otherwise the only new aircraft added was a pair of A300-600Rs in 1994 and these were only allowed as part of the United States' compensation payment for the downing of Iran Air Flight 655 by the US Navy.[3]

Notwithstanding Iran's status as a pariah state and its subsequent isolation, liberalisation of the aviation scene saw new airlines appear as the 1980s turned into the 1990s. This was the result of the ceasefire with Iraq. Demand for air travel enormously increased while the two leading state-owned airlines (Iran Air and Aseman) were not able to meet demand. Therefore, some entrepreneurs and even government agencies, interested in having a share in the lucrative air travel market, grabbed the opportunity to lobby the government with suggestions to make up for the capacity shortage. As a result, the government decided to abolish Iran Air's monopoly and it relaxed the policy of awarding operating permits for start-up airlines. Saha Air Lines was formed by the Iranian Air Force, using ex-air force Boeing 707s. Private airlines were also set up, including Caspian Airlines, Kish Airlines and Mahan Air (which would become Iran Air's main competitor). Caspian and Kish started services with Yakovlev Yak-42Ds, acquired via Russian and Ukrainian airlines. Mahan Air, which would grow to become one of Iran's largest airlines, started operations with Russian Tupolev Tu-154s, just like Iran Air's subsidiary Iran Airtour had done. Russian aircraft would form an increasingly important part of the Iranian fleet because they could be obtained from the Russians, thus avoiding sanctions imposed on selling aircraft with American parts to Iran.[4] Nevertheless, Iran Air also managed to buy some Fokker 100 aircraft from its Dutch manufacturer. But other parties were also willing to circumvent American sanctions. Iran Air managed to buy four second-hand Airbus B2s and B4s in Turkey. Thirteen Fokker 100s were bought from Brazilian carrier TAM Linhas Aéreas through the establishment of intermediary companies.

Owing to the start-up of several new airlines, domestic air transportation was greatly expanded and more destinations were served, flight frequencies increased and more passengers were carried. This hasty expansion produced chaos in the country's air transport sector and stagnated the whole industry's improvement. Airlines became competitors, not only when they wanted to increase their passenger numbers, but also when buying spare parts. As such, parts were difficult to obtain due to sanctions against Iran, and a black market developed. In the absence of the government's adequate laws, regulations and policies to standardise and control airline operations, the airlines' most important features – aircraft, crew and passenger safety – were totally jeopardised and the quality of service diminished. Consequently, the country was witnessing incidents, air disasters, loss of human life and the travelling public's total dissatisfaction. Iran Air lost its pre-revolution grandeur. However, this was not only the result of the American sanctions and the war but also Iran Air adopting the wrong strategies and making wrong decisions, or no decisions at all.

One of the flag carrier's first major problems after the revolution was the impossibility of knowledgeable and experienced general managers continuing their service in office. Instead, they were replaced every few months by unprofessional people who were unfamiliar with the sophisticated airline business and its problems. These people – put in place by the government – needed plenty of time to be trained on the job and would have been talented enough to learn, but before they could do so, they were replaced before being given the opportunity to put their knowledge to work.[5]

A similar problem occurred at a lower-level management. The sudden loss of a large number of valuable, experienced and educated managers, each specialists in their own right, was a catastrophe for Iran Air. The collective dismissal for unsubstantiated and fake political reasons by so-called purging committees (which later proved to be entirely unfounded and unjustified) was extremely destructive and irreversible.

In the meantime, Iran Airtour also had to adapt to the changing environment, as the airline – the subsidiary of Iran Air – was mainly intended to follow the strategic and economic policies of Iran Air. Due to the revolution, the Iranian travelling public's appetite was switching from entertaining journeys in Western and European countries to Islamic countries. Iran Airtour made an effort to meet this new goal. Whereas in the early years of its operations the airline had used Boeing 737 equipment, leased from Iran Air, it now operated Tupolev Tu-154s on lease from Russia. In 1992, Iran Airtour was appointed by Iran Air to use the Tupolevs to support passenger transportation on domestic routes. Some international routes, like the flights to Damascus, Almaty, Moscow, Ashgabat and Tashkent, were also assigned by Iran Air to Iran Airtour to enhance the operational capacity of Iran Air's limited fleet.

The Shah of Iran – seen here upon his arrival in Budapest – often used Iran Air on his state visits. (Fortepan)

When the revolution in Iran started, Iran Air had several Boeing 707s like this 707-300 in its fleet. (Thijs Postma)

In 1977, Iran Air leased this Boeing 707-321C from Pan Am for a very short period of time. (Alan Bushell)

At the time of the revolution, Iran Air also had Boeing 727s in its fleet. (ETH Bibliothek Zürich)

With the Boeing 747SP, Iran Air could operate flights from Tehran to New York. (Alejandro Hernández León)

This Iran Air Boeing 747SP is seen here at Narita Airport. (Intele, public domain, via Wikimedia Commons)

This Boeing 747-100 was delivered in August 1979 during the Iranian Revolution. (Friedrich Wieser)

This Boeing 747-200 was delivered in 1977, direct from the factory. (Arpingstone, public domain, via Wikimedia Commons)

Notwithstanding the sanctions against Iran, this Airbus A300-600 EP-IBA was able to be delivered by Airbus Industries to the airline in 1994 as compensation for the Airbus A300 (EP-IBU), which was shot down by American forces over the Persian Gulf. (Alf van Beem, CC0, via Wikimedia Commons)

Airbus A300-600 EP – IBB was also delivered new from the factory as compensation for EP-IBU. (Jozef Mols)

This Fokker 100 – seen here at Birjand Airport – was obtained second-hand in 1991. (Aabedii, CC BY-SA 3.0 https://creativecommons.org/licenses/by-sa/3.0, via Wikimedia Commons)

Iran Air's subsidiary, Iran Airtour, started its operations with a fleet of Tupolev Tu-154Ms (Waka77, Public domain, via Wikimedia Commons)

An Iran Airtour TU-154 at Tabriz Airport. (Hansueli Krapf, CC BY-SA 3.0 https://creativecommons.org/licenses/by-sa/3.0, via Wikimedia Commons)

**Besides Iran Airtour, competitor Kish Air also started up operations with Tupolev Tu-154s. (Jozef Mols)**

**By buying Russian equipment, competitor Kish Air could – just like Iran Airtour – circumvent American sanctions. (Jozef Mols)**

**Competitor Caspian also used the Tupolev Tu-154. (Jozef Mols)**

**By buying more Soviet-made aircraft, like this Yakovlev Yak-42, Caspian also circumvented American sanctions. (Jozef Mols)**

# Chapter 6

# Creativity and Self-sufficiency

Prior to the revolution, Iran Air had been a very good customer for American aircraft manufacturers. Therefore, it also brought hundreds of Western expatriates to Iran to oversee maintenance and engineering operations. When the Shah of Iran was overthrown, and Ayatollah Khomeini came to power, relations with the US were frozen. Even years after the release of the American hostages from the American Embassy in Tehran, no official diplomatic relations existed between the two countries. At that time, Iran Air transported some 1.7 million passengers per year, but airline reservation systems in North America, which were accessed for flights to Iran, were flagged with a State Department warning against travel to that country.[1] As for maintenance, on average 1,000–1,400 expatriates performed light maintenance, but all intermediate and heavy work was carried out abroad. When the expatriates left Iran after the revolution, they had to be replaced. Furthermore, the US government had imposed sanctions so Iran Air was no longer able to obtain spare parts and keep flying. To school Iranians in the jobs previously held by foreigners, the airline decided to build a training centre at Tehran's Mehrabad Airport. This way, dependence on services by foreign workers decreased and, at the same time, the airline was able to offer jobs to Iranian nationals. According to Iran Air, almost all of the narrow-body maintenance and some 80 per cent of the widebody work could be performed in house, including full D-checks. The avionics shop was able to repair more then 90 per cent of the electronic components and engine work was also performed at the Tehran base.[2] As the airline was not eager to recruit former air force pilots, it started an ab initio training programme, using Boeing 707 and 727 Singer Link simulators. In the meantime, Iran Air had also changed its formal name to 'The Airline of the Islamic Republic of Iran', although this name change was not reflected in the logos on its jets.

Notwithstanding the efforts to become self-sufficient, Iran Air could not ignore the fact that its fleet was becoming obsolete, and airframe replacement became a major concern. With the American embargo, buying American aircraft had become impossible. As several Iranian airlines had been obtaining aircraft in the Soviet Union, Iran Air was eying the Antonov TU-334 passenger jet and even hoped to set up a production plant in Isfahan, where the jets could be built under licence. But development of the TU-334 did not go further than the construction and demonstration of a prototype, after which Tupolev decided to stop the project. Another possibility was the production under licence of the Antonov An-140 50-seater. (Later, some of these aircraft would indeed be assembled in Iran, but they were never used by Iran Air.) Obtaining new aircraft became so urgent for Iran Air that the Iranian government even started negotiations with Fokker over a possible rescue of the bankrupt Dutch aircraft builder. Due to improved relations between the Islamic Republic of Iran and Europe during the presidency of Mohammad Khatami, Iran Air was able to finalise a contract for the purchase of several Airbus A330-300 aircraft, but the deal was cancelled by Airbus under pressure from the US State Department. Iran Air only managed to buy five second-hand Airbus A310-200s and a single Airbus A310-300 from Turkey, followed by two also second-hand Airbus A300-600s from Greek carrier Olympic Airlines. Some of the Turkish aircraft had to be stored soon after as it was impossible to source spare parts for the engines.

Although Iranian airlines had large fleets of aircraft, more than 100 of them (some owned by Iran Air) had to be grounded due to lack of access to new parts and technical expertise following the sanctions imposed by Western countries. The prolonged period of time that Iran Air was under international sanctions had led to a dramatic rise in the average fleet age and plunging safety records. Iran Air became known as one of the worst airlines in the world in terms of air safety records. Technical problems with the aircraft also led to public anger and frustration among the passengers because of the many flight delays and cancellations. Often, these protests took the form of violent confrontations with the airline employees and aeroplane sit-ins for many hours after a severely delayed flight had finally landed.

In an initial attempt to limit Iran Air's flights over the European Union (EU), some European countries refused to refuel Iranian passenger jets. This move followed unilateral sanctions imposed by the United States over the nuclear weapons dispute. On 5 July 2010, an aviation official of Iran accused the UK, Germany and the United Arab Emirates of refusing to refuel Iranian aircraft. Both Iran Air and Mahan Air claimed to have been denied refuelling. A spokesperson for the United Kingdom Civil Aviation Authority said it was the sole decision of independent suppliers if aircraft were to be refuelled or not. Germany's Transport Ministry said the refuelling of Iranian aircraft was not banned under EU or UN sanctions, but he did not say whether any independent refuellers were denying fuel. Later the same day, Dubai Airport revealed that it was continuing to refuel Iranian passenger flights in and out of Dubai.[3,4,5] Unilateral American sanctions against Iran – signed by President Barack Obama – prohibited the sale or provision to Iran of refined petroleum products worth more than US$5m (£3.3m) per year. In the meantime, the Iranian foreign minister had refuted claims that foreign countries had denied refuelling to Iranian flights and stated the false report was part of a 'psychological war' against Tehran.[6] To avoid refuelling problems, Iran Air decided its aircraft would take off from Iran with a maximum fuel load. On the way home, they would make a technical stop to refuel. This would usually be in Istanbul, Budapest or Belgrade.[7]

On 6 July 2010, it was announced that the European Commission would ban all of Iran Air's Airbus A300s, Boeing 727s and Boeing 747s – two-thirds of Iran Air's fleet – from the EU over safety concerns. In 2008, Saeed Hesami, the then CEO of Iran Air, had said the EU had already made a decision and was working hard to pave the way for the suspension of all Iran Air flights to and from Europe.[8] When the EU issued its ban, it stressed immediately that the ban was on safety grounds and not related to sanctions imposed on Iran because of its nuclear programme, which the government in Tehran claimed was for peaceful purposes.[9]

Sanctions against Iran went much further than refusing to refuel aircraft or banning aircraft types from European skies. Iranian civilian aviation had been subject to unilateral and international restrictions due to its operational habits of using aircraft interchangeably for civilian passenger flights and military related activities. Iranian aircraft had transported weapons and military personnel outside the country, especially in times of conflict in the Middle East. As a result, Iran Air was mentioned in both United Nations Security Council (UNSC) Resolutions 1803 (2008) and 1929 (2010) as an entity whose air cargo to and from Iran should be inspected by member states. In this respect, if they suspected UNSC restrictive measures were violated, including reregistering or renaming aircraft, such violations should be communicated to the UN. In July 2010, restrictions were imposed at a regional level by the EU. Cargo flights operated by Iranian carriers or originating from Iran were banned from accessing EU airports.[10]

Although most of the sanctions against Iran – with the exception of the EU's ban of Iran Air's older aircraft types – were inspired by political motives rather than by security concerns, Iran Air itself also realised the use of older aircraft types increased safety risks. In January 2011, the Iranian authorities announced they would introduce a ban on all Russian Tupolev aircraft, starting in February 2011. This decision came in connection with the increasing number of incidents involving these aircraft on the territory of Iran itself. Furthermore, Iranian airlines would no longer employ foreign pilots, unfamiliar with the topography of the country. Russian pilots of civilian aircraft, working in the Islamic Republic, were given two months to leave the country. At the time of the announcement, Iran Airtour, Kish Air, Eram and Taban airlines had a combined fleet of 19 Tupolev Tu-154s. The decision by the government also included a ban on other Russian-made aircraft, including the Ilyushin Il-62s of Aria Airlines. As buying modern Western aircraft was impossible, Iran Air – and other Iranian airlines – became forced to lease foreign aircraft to continue flying.[11, 12] Nevertheless, the airline managed to obtain second-hand aircraft from abroad. In 2011, Iran Air succeeded in purchasing three Boeing 747-300s from Qantas Airlines through an intermediate company. The aircraft, however, already had an average life of 25 years. After the arrival of the first aircraft, the American government tried to prevent delivery of the two other aircraft. But in the end, Iran Air decided not to use the aircraft due to its inability to obtain spare parts for it. Several other Boeing 747s belonging to Iran Air were removed from the active fleet in the next few years. When it was clear that buying Boeing 737s – even via intermediate companies – was impossible, Iran Air decided to obtain a series of Fokker 100s, as the aircraft, equipped with British Rolls-Royce engines, had no American parts. Disappointed with the slow impact of the sanctions on Iran's Fokker deals, the American government pressured all airlines using the aircraft type to scrap Fokker 100s and all their parts immediately after retirement so they would not fall into the hands of Iran.

American pressure continued in an effort to boycott Iran. In June 2011, Iran Air had to terminate its use of Belgrade and Ljubljana airports as a refuelling base for flights originating from Western Europe en route to Tehran. Most Iran Air flights from London previously made a refuelling stop in Ljubljana on their way to Tehran. Refuelling stops in Belgrade were mostly for flights originating in Germany. This practice came to an end after the United States issued an advisory to all airports in Europe to stop refuelling all Iran Air jets. Although the Belgrade and Ljubljana airports had made significant profits out of their arrangement with the Iranian carrier, they had to give in to American diplomatic pressure. The American advisory was based on a statement that Revolutionary Guard officers were said to occasionally take control of Iran Air flights with special cargo. However, Belgrade Airport would provide services to Iran Air again in late 2013. Earlier, the United States had also intervened in a deal between Adria Airways and the Iranian airline Yas Air. When, in 2011, Adria wanted to sell its Airbus A320 to Yas, it received a stern warning from the United States to immediately halt such plans.[13]

When the British Embassy in Tehran and the Iranian Embassy in London were closed, Manston Airport also decided to stop refuelling Iran Air flights. Iran Air was able to land at Heathrow but could not refuel its aircraft, because US sanctions prevented Iran Air dealing with companies that had links to America. Manston, owned by Infratil, had no such American trade connections and could, therefore, continue to offer refuelling services. However, tensions between the UK and Iran put an end to this refuelling service in December 2011.[14]

Iran Air's maintenance department at Tehran Mehrabad Airport. (Iran Air)

This Airbus A300-600 – seen here in Amsterdam – was obtained second-hand from Olympic Airlines in 2005. (Jozef Mols)

**Airbus A300 aircraft like this one, obtained second-hand from Turkish Airlines, only remained in the fleet for a short while as it was impossible to source spare parts for the engines. (Dara Zarbaf)**

**Iran Air obtained this second-hand Airbus A310 in 2000. (Alan Bushell)**

**When this Boeing 747 EP-ICD was no longer in use as a passenger plane, it was used in the cargo role. (Firat Cimenli)**

The same Boeing 747 EP-ICD in its cargo role. (Hansueli Krapf, CC BY-SA 3.0 https://creativecommons.org/licenses/by-sa/3.0, via Wikimedia Commons)

As the Fokker 100 had British engines and was made in Holland, it was easier to obtain this aircraft type on the second-hand market as American sanctions did not apply. (Aabedii, CC BY-SA 3.0 https://creativecommons.org/licenses/by-sa/3.0, via Wikimedia Commons)

## Creativity and Self-sufficiency

As it was difficult for Iran Air to buy aircraft, it had to lease some, like this McDonnell Douglas MD-83 from Cham Wings in Syria. (Hansueli Krapf, CC BY-SA 3.0 https://creativecommons.org/licenses/by-sa/3.0, via Wikimedia Commons)

As Iran Air could not obtain new aircraft, this Airbus A320 was leased from Armenian carrier Vertir Airlines. (Dara Zarbaf)

# Chapter 7
# Improved Relations

The 2005 Iranian presidential elections brought conservative populist candidate Mahmoud Ahmadinejad to power. When he was re-elected in 2009, the results of the elections were widely disputed and resulted in widespread protest, both within Iran and among Iranian communities outside the country. On 15 June 2013, Hassan Rouhani was elected as president. His electoral victory would, to some extent, improve Iran's relations with the rest of the world.

In the meantime, and notwithstanding the problems Iranian carriers experienced when sourcing new aircraft or spare parts, demand for air travel by Iranians had gone up. In the ten years between 2006 and 2016, passenger traffic doubled at Iranian airports. If one compares the situation with that in Turkey, which has similar fundamentals, the size of the Iranian aircraft fleet was only one-third of its Turkish counterpart. The market had also been further liberalised by the Civil Aviation Organisation of Iran. By December 2015, 170 domestic routes had been deregulated to create more competition between airlines, and these routes included important services to the popular Kish and Qeshm Islands. The remaining 87 routes were deregulated by the end of March 2016. Many of the new start-up carriers had seemingly thrived despite operational limitations as a result of Western sanctions. However, two of them encountered problems. Sepahan Airlines was set up as an internal division of the Iran Aircraft Manufacturing Industrial Company (HESA) and operated a fleet of Antonov An-140 turboprops, which were manufactured under licence by HESA. But when one of them crashed, the airline's fleet was grounded. Atrak Air was another start-up that would not last for long. Iran Air, Iran Aseman and Mahan Air clearly dominated the domestic market, with a market share of 56 per cent, spread evenly between them. Where international traffic is concerned, about 70 per cent was carried by Iranian carriers with, once again, Mahan and Iran Air dominating the market.[1]

President Rouhani had opened the door for negotiations between Western countries and Iran regarding the reduction of Iran's nuclear capabilities. On 16 January 2016, Iran satisfied the conditions of the JCPOA Accord (Joint Comprehensive Plan of Action) agreed the previous July to reduce its nuclear capabilities. This allowed for the removal and rollback of a wide range of sanctions against Iran, including those that stopped the sale of new passenger aircraft to most Iranian carriers, plus services associated with warranty, maintenance, repair and safety related issues.[2] On 15 January 2016, President Obama authorised his secretary of state, John Kerry, to lift all sanctions on Iran's civil aviation. With the start of the agreement's implementation, this led to the resumption of refuelling of Iran Air aircraft at most European destinations. Sweden, however, continued to refuse Iran Air refuelling at Stockholm and Gothenburg. In anticipation of the JCPOA deal being reached, the president of Iran Air, Farhad Parvaresh, had stated the airline would then seek to obtain at least 100 widebody and short-haul jets from Western manufacturers, including Boeing and Airbus. Regional aircraft would be obtained from Bombardier and Embraer. The chair continued his statement by saying his airline was expected to spend some US$3–5bn when purchasing the new equipment[3] but, in reality, the amount was many times higher. During the years of the Western ban, MRO (maintenance, repair and operations) costs amounted to about 25 per cent of the Iranian airlines' costs compared to 10–15 per cent in the rest of the world. Obtaining new equipment was, therefore, of the utmost importance. Iran Air indicated that about 60 of its aircraft could be returned to service once parts necessary for overhaul were made available from Western manufacturers. But putting these aircraft back into the sky would be a strictly short-term measure to meet demand while Iran Air was waiting for the delivery of new aircraft.

As could be expected, Western airframe manufacturers were quick to court Iranian airlines. It soon became known that Iran Air was in negotiations with Airbus for the delivery of up to 100 aircraft. Obtaining parts and new aircraft was one of the challenges. When the Western bans ended, Iran Air employed about 7,000 workers, roughly 200 per aircraft. This figure was in line with its regional competitors. If Iran Air wanted to expand its fleet to 120 aircraft, it would have to increase its workforce to around 20,000. And, of course, the airline would have to adapt its technical infrastructure to deal with the new aircraft types that would soon join the fleet. Airbus – hoping to receive a mega-order from the Iranian carrier – made it clear it was willing to provide assistance for airport and aircraft operations and training in the maintenance and repair operations. Furthermore, Airbus hoped to take advantage of the fact that US sanctions were more involved than the European sanctions and that it would take longer to unwind, meaning Boeing would need to be patient before any deal with Iran Air could be announced and finalised. While the hunt for the 'deal of the century' was going on between Airbus and Boeing, manufacturers of smaller regional aircraft like Embraer, Bombardier and Mitsubishi each made their proposals as well.[4]

Besides the choice of new aircraft types for its fleet, Iran Air had to look into the possible funding for such purchases. Japan had relinquished its sanctions against Iran on 21 January 2016 and Canada followed its example shortly afterwards. Brazil never enacted sanctions against Iran, but exports were blocked due to American sanction rules about the exports of aircraft containing American parts. In Europe, Italy and France played important roles through the participation of their export credit agencies Sace (Italy) and Coface (France) in the financing of the ATR deal. And, of course, lessors and Chinese banks were willing to provide an alternative for American and European financing.

Obtaining funding for the purchase of new aircraft was only one aspect of the financing of the new deals. Iran never signed the Cape Town Convention, which protects the interests of aircraft lessors and owners by guaranteeing rights concerning aircraft ownership, defaults on leases, recouping debts and repossessing aircraft. Therefore, Iran stated in January 2016 that it had started the process to join the convention in order to facilitate the leasing of aircraft from foreign owners – a process that takes time.[5]

On 28 January 2016, Airbus issued a statement saying that an agreement had been signed with Iran Air regarding the purchase of 118 new aircraft, spanning from Airbus' single-aisle A320 product line – involving both current engine option (ceo) and new engine option (neo) options – to the widebody A330 ceo and A330 neo family jetliners. Covered in the agreement were 21 A320 ceo and 24 A320 neo aircraft, 27 A330 ceo, 18 A330-900 neos, 16 A350-1000s and 12 A380s. While phasing in this major new inventory, Iran Air would be supported by Airbus' extensive resources in the fields of pilot and maintenance training, customer support and services. The deal was signed at the Elysée Palace in Paris in the presence of Iranian president Hassan Rouhani and French president François Hollande.[6] The deal for a total of 118 Airbus aircraft was valued at approximately US$25bn (£19.4bn).[7] A few days earlier, Iran Air had started to refuel its planes in Paris Orly. Shortly after the signing of the Airbus order, ATR announced that Iran had agreed to buy up to 40 ATR-72-600 turboprop aircraft. The deal included firm orders for 20 aircraft and options for 20 more, financed through the French and Italian export credit agencies.[8] However, negotiations dragged on over an agreement for maintenance and spare engines between Iran Air and engine supplier Pratt & Whitney Canada (which is owned by the American aerospace group United Technologies). But by April 2017, the deal was finalised.[9] In the meantime, Iran Air had received its first Airbus aircraft from the 100-aircraft Airbus order when, in January 2017, the first Airbus A321 landed at Tehran Mehrabad Airport. Soon, it was being used on both domestic and regional routes. Delivery of two Airbus A330s was expected for February 2017.[10] On 17 May 2017, Mehrabad Airport saw the touchdown of four new ATR-72-600 aircraft for Iran Air.[11]

Anticipating the arrival of the new aircraft in 2017, Iran Air was set to send Iranian pilgrims to the Hajj in Saudi Arabia. The previous year, this had been impossible due to deepening tensions between the two nations. A total of 86,000 Iranian pilgrims were expected to participate in the pilgrimage in 2017, leaving from 20 Iranian airports. The share of flights was originally divided equally between Saudi Arabia and Iran; however, Iran Airports Company reported that Saudi Arabia had reduced its share to 30 per cent. Iran's 70 per cent share was fully claimed by Iran Air. The airline clearly indicated it would not use the new Airbus aircraft on the Hajj flights. Arrival of the new aircraft would liberate old aircraft from the Iran Air fleet to operate the pilgrim flights. This announcement came from Iran Air's newly appointed chair and managing director, Farzaneh Sharafbafi – the first woman to hold this important position within the airline.[12] She was also the first Iranian woman to receive a PhD in aerospace and had been on the board of Iran Air for several years. During her inaugural speech, she announced 'a comprehensive renovation and restructuring of the airline'. She also thanked her predecessor, Farhad Parvaresh, who had led the airline for more than eight years, a period he described as the hardest years for the flag carrier: his term had coincided with the toughest international sanctions against Iran.[13] Sharafbafi also announced that Iran Air was to launch a new subsidiary airline to regional destinations under the brand name 'IranAir Regional'. The new service would be launched alongside the newly delivered ATR-72 equipment.[14]

Farzaneh Sharafbafi became the first female CEO of Iran Air. (Iran Air)

Farad Parvaresh, who had guided Iran Air through difficult times. (Iran Air)

The new ATR aircraft are presented to the press. (Jozef Mols collection)

Two new ATR 72 aircraft in the Iran Air hangar. (Iran Air)

A new ATR 72 arrives in front of the obsolete Iran Air fleet. (Sadra Mosala/Iran Air)

The new ATRs are shown to the public in the Iran Air hangar. (Iran Air)

The new ATR equipment was immediately put into service on domestic routes and into neighbouring countries. (Dara Zarbaf)

The arrival of the first new Airbus A321 opens new perspectives for Iran Air. (Iran Air)

Iran Air's first Airbus A321 was immediately used on regional routes. (Dara Zarbaf)

When – after the boycott of Iran – new spare parts arrived, this Fokker 100, which had been grounded for years without engines and landing gear, was fully restored and returned to the sky. (Iran Air)

## Chapter 8
# The American Connection

When a series of sanctions against Iran was lifted in 2016, Iranian airlines started negotiations with aircraft manufacturers in order to modernise their fleets as soon as possible. One might have thought Iranian carriers would turn to Airbus in the first place and ignore Boeing. Most of the past sanctions had indeed been imposed under pressure from the United States, which was still seen as 'the land of evil' by the Iranian government. But Iranian airlines – and especially Iran Air – remained rather neutral in their selection of suppliers. They not only ordered aircraft from Airbus but also started talks with Boeing.

On 11 December 2016, it became known that Iran Air had signed a US$16.6bn (£13.2bn) deal with the American aircraft manufacturer Boeing, covering 50 narrowbody 737 MAX aircraft, and 30 long-haul 777s, split equally between the 777-300ER (which was badly in need of an order boost at that time) and the 406-seat 777-9, which was still under development.[1] The delivery of the aircraft was spread over a ten-year period. The Boeing contract, the biggest Iran–American deal since the fall of the Shah, was supposed to clear major technical hurdles towards the implementation of the pact between Iran and world powers to reopen trade in return for curbs on Iran's nuclear activities. Besides Iran Air, Iran Aseman had also ordered some Boeing 737 jets.

The Boeing deal, however, remained uncertain. From the beginning, Republicans in the US Congress tried to counter the nuclear deal. At the same time, the American House of Representatives passed a bill seeking to restrict financial transactions by American banks in an effort to block the sale of Western passenger jets to Iran. Iran immediately made it clear it was still negotiating with 'third parties' to arrange the financing of the deal, but added that money from the deal would not pass through the American financial system. About 85 per cent of the US$16.6bn Boeing order would be financed through 'foreign sources', whereas the rest would be paid in cash by Iran Air. Iran Air's 15 per cent payment would be sourced from Iran's sovereign wealth fund. This National Development Fund of Iran (NDFI) had been created in 2011 to save oil revenues, to develop Iran and invest overseas for future generations. Under Iranian law, the government had to deposit 20 per cent of all oil revenue to NDFI. According to the fund's deputy for economic affairs, Mohammad Saeed Nouri Nacini, the NDFI had amassed US$67bn in deposits since its inception.[2]

It was clear to everybody that, whereas President Obama had proudly defended the nuclear deal with Iran, other politicians in the United States (and abroad) tried to use all means available to sabotage Iranian trade with the West. One of those people was the then president-elect, Donald Trump, who had opposed the lifting of sanctions against Iran. It was clear that, even if the American government would issue American export licences regarding the Boeing deal with Iran, such licences might have to be extended under the Trump administration as they only had limited validity, whereas the Iran Air order had a length of ten years. In September and November 2016, the American export control authority, the Treasury Department's Office of Foreign Asset Controls (OFAC), issued export licences for both Airbus and Boeing (at the time, Barack Obama was still president). These certificates would remain valid until 2020 and would, therefore, have to be extended until delivery of the last ordered aircraft.[3]

Boeing had defended the Iran deal by stating the contract would fund tens of thousands of jobs for the 777-300ER jets and nearly 100,000 aerospace jobs for the whole package. The easing of sanctions against Iran had come at a crucial moment for the aerospace industry as many unsold aircraft had been parked with the manufacturers. Iran's return to the world economy was helping aircraft manufacturers cope with a downturn in global demand, providing homes for aircraft, orphaned by reversals in growth plans of airlines elsewhere. Despite denials by manufacturers that the downturn was hurting, Iran's return to the market brought to light pockets of surplus aircraft.[4]

Shortly after the signing of Iran's order, Boeing had offered Iran Air two Boeing 747-800 jets. The aircraft had originally been built for Russia's OJSC Transaero Airlines, which went bankrupt in 2015. Boeing was eager to include the planes in the contract secured with Iran Air in December 2016, even at dumping prices. But Iran Air refused the offer. The airline's strategy was based on the introduction of 777s, Airbus A330s and A350s. The 747-800 was not a type Iran Air wanted, considering its fleet expansion plan.[5] The 747-800 was not the only deal Iran Air refused. Earlier, Iran Air confirmed the cancellation of the earlier-than-expected delivery of a Boeing 777-300ER as part of the order with Boeing. The cancellation came after deputy minister of roads and urban development, Asghar Fakhrieh Kashan, announced that Boeing had offered the jet to Iran Air after Turkish Airlines had cancelled its order ahead of delivery. He stated that Iran Air refused the offer as there were 'too many difficulties' to be solved. Firstly, as the Boeing 777 would have been delivered much earlier than indicated in the Iran Air order, the airline had not yet secured the necessary funds to take delivery of the jet. On the other hand, it was very likely that Turkish Airlines would take delivery of this TC-LJK anyhow as the carrier had already paid millions in pre-delivery payments. And finally, the aircraft ordered by Turkish Airlines did not have exactly the same specifications as the 777s ordered by Iran Air.[6] In the meantime, Iran Air had also decided to drop preliminary plans to take 12 Airbus A380s – a decision that was being marked as a new blow to the A380 order book. As Tehran was – and would remain – a small hub in the short-term, and irrespective of whether Iran Air could find sustainable markets for the type, by the time Iran Air had planned to receive its first A380, the type would have been well into its mid-life, with dwindling spare parts and support.[7]

When President Trump took office in January 2018, it became obvious that the aviation deal with Iran was in danger. Trump, who had strongly criticised the 2015 deal to lift a raft of sanctions in return for restrictions on Iran's nuclear activities, urged European allies to help fix what he called 'disastrous flaws' in the pact… or face an American exit.[8] In response, Airbus sales chief John Leahy told Reuters in an interview that he thought the deals would get fulfilled but maybe not to the original schedule.[9] Bankers said further business with Iran had been held up by the reluctance of Western financial institutions to deal with Tehran because of concerns the nuclear deal could unravel or that they could fall foul of ongoing American financial controls. These concerns hampered the financing of aircraft deliveries to Iran Air, which had to look for other means of financing the deal.

In May 2018, President Trump's scrapping of the Iran nuclear deal, his imposition of new sanctions and his revoking of previously delivered export licences completely killed the prospect of Boeing delivering jets to Iran. But, given Trump's hawkish views on Iran before he took office, Boeing always had seen the deals as tenuous. It had not delivered any aeroplanes and never firmly booked the orders, although it had tried to 'dump' a few surplus aircraft in the Iranian market. 'We have no Iranian deliveries that are scheduled,' Boeing stated. In contrast, Airbus had formally added the ordered aircraft to its order book and had even rushed to deliver the first aeroplanes as soon as it had become legal. That way, since the lifting of sanctions under the Obama administration, Airbus had delivered three jets – one A321 and two leased A330s – to Iran Air. Another eight 'white tail' ATR-72s had also been quickly delivered to the Iranian carrier by ATR.[10] After the announcement of the new sanctions under the Trump administration, Airbus spokesperson Mary Anne Greczy said the company was 'carefully analysing the President's announcement and would be evaluating next steps. But Airbus would remain in full compliance with American sanctions and export control regulations.'[11] While the Airbus deal was not necessarily totally dead, prospects for filling it were 'not great'. To be able to deliver the ordered aircraft and, at the same time, comply with American sanctions, Airbus would have to replace American components in the aircraft with components from neutral countries. In the long run, however, Airbus might just benefit from Europe's less fraught relationship with Iran. Airbus might even take a greater market share in Iran in the future, considering the strong relationships between the European and Iranian governments.

The new sanctions against Iran not only affected Iran Air but also other Iranian airlines, including Iran Airtour, Aseman Airlines, Qeshm Air (which had ordered ten Boeing 737 MAX aircraft as well as five Boeing 737-800s) and Kish Air.[12] In the United States, Boeing also experienced the 'fallout' of Trump's decisions. But after a short visit to Saudi Arabia, the American president announced he had signed contracts there for American companies like Boeing, valued at US$110bn (£87.5bn). This was good news for Boeing (and other American companies), but also for Saudi Arabia, as the Sunni Muslim rulers there had taken a dim view of the earlier lifting of sanctions against Iran – a Shi'ite Muslim-majority theocracy – under the Obama administration. It is not clear whether Saudi Arabia had 'influenced' or 'convinced' Trump to kill the Boeing/Airbus deal with Tehran, but this cannot be excluded.

As soon as sanctions were lifted, Iran received its first Airbus A330. (Alireza Izadi/Iran Air)

The Airbus A330-200 was the only large aircraft Iran Air could obtain after the lifting of sanctions. (Iran Air)

An Iran Airbus A330-200 seen upon arrival in Tehran. (Iran Air)

This Airbus is being prepared for its next flight. (Iran Air)

The economy cabin of the new Airbus A330. (Iran Air)

Homa class (business class) in the new Airbus A330. (Iran Air)

Homa-class service. (Iran Air)

Notwithstanding all sanctions, Iran Air had to keep its Airbus A300 in flying condition. (Iran Air)

The 747s also had to be kept in flying condition. (Iran Air)

# Chapter 9
# The Consequences

In the few months following the lifting of international sanctions, Iran had set about what amounted to a complete overhaul of its aviation sector. Its airlines had placed orders for more than 300 new aircraft and options for a further 50 planes. Of course, Iran Air had been the most active buyer. It had placed orders and options for 220 new planes from Airbus, Boeing and ATR. Among the country's smaller carriers, Iran Aseman Airlines had lined up 30 new Boeing 737 MAX 8 jets, with options for 30 more. Iran Airtour had signed a memorandum of understanding for 45 Airbus A320 neo aircraft, whereas Zagros Airlines had signed one for 28 Airbus aircraft, including 20 A320 neos and eight A330 neos. Iran Air's first A320 arrived in January 2017 and an A330 was delivered in March of the same year. In May, the first ATR-72-600 touched down at Tehran's airport.[1]

Iran Air had hoped to earn US$1bn to $1.2bn (£800m to £950m) per year from ticket sales once all the planes it had ordered over the past months had been delivered. With this amount, Iran Air would have been able to repay the instalments for the aircraft it had bought. Aircraft, which had already been delivered before the new embargo against the country, had been pre-financed by their manufacturers. But the prospect of financing the rest of the planes remained difficult as major banks and big financial institutions were hesitant to engage with Iran, fearing American penalties.[2] While the Trump administration was working on a full boycott of the Iranian aviation industry, China agreed to finance the delivery of a few Airbus aircraft to Iran Air.

Iran Air was fully owned by the state. In the past, officials had voiced the possibility of listing the company on both the Tehran Stock Exchange as well as international equity markets. With the introduction of a new American boycott, the idea of privatising Iran Air was far removed, however. In 2021, after Iran Air was hit by the Covid pandemic, which severely impacted its financial results, the long-expected privatisation of the flag carrier was cancelled completely.

If new jets had been introduced, this would have had to be matched with new routes and greater connectivity and codeshare pacts so that travellers would have more options beyond Iran Air's network. Without new routes, deploying the planned 200 new aircraft would be difficult. It would hamper earnings and lead to greater costs.[3]

The re-establishment of sanctions by the US, however, not only stopped the delivery of new aircraft, but also, once again, cut off Iranian airlines' access to parts and technical services, needed to keep older aircraft in the air. With sanctions stopping the purchase of any new aircraft with more than 10 per cent of American-made parts, even the Sukhoi SSJ100 Superjet became unobtainable. In an interview with Financialtribune.com, Ali Asghar Fakrieh Kashan (an adviser to the minister of roads and urban development) stated Iran Air had no plan to renovate its fleet with Russian-made Sukhoi jets. He also denied he had received a proposal for bartering such jets with oil, referring to rumours that had spread in Tehran.[4]

The unilateral revocation of export licences by the US Treasury Department created an unprecedented situation. The United States had been one of the signatories of the nuclear deal with Iran, together with five other nations, but the USA was the only party involved to leave the agreement, whereas the other signatories remained committed to the pact. As European aircraft, ordered by Iran, contained more than 10 per cent of American-made parts, the USA made it impossible for European manufacturers to deliver the ordered planes to Iran. Under a special agreement after US licences were revoked, but before new sanctions came into force, ATR decided to deliver 13 of the 20 turboprop aircraft sought by Iran Air. About US$70m (£56m), needed to finance the purchase of ATR aircraft, was raised via a bonds issue in Iran.[5] Airbus, which had delivered three aircraft before the licences were withdrawn, continued to show the Iran Air order as active on its books.[6]

As Iran Air was not in a position to obtain new aircraft anymore, it had to rejuvenate its fleet in a different manner. In February 2019, the airline managed to add three second-hand Airbus A319 jets to its fleet. The aircraft were obtained from an unnamed domestic airline that had bought the aircraft in 2002. This measure was necessary to increase capacity on flights to meet the high seasonal demand for air travel during the Iranian New Year, starting in March.[7] The airline also overhauled a 25-year-old Fokker 100, which had been grounded for over two years for lack of landing gear and engines. A delivery of spare parts, just before the American embargo against Iran, had made it possible to return the aircraft to the fleet.[8] To further expand its fleet, Iran Air once again leased aircraft abroad. From Bukovyna airlines in Ukraine, the carrier obtained several McDonnell Douglas MD 82s. Iran Air's subsidiary, Iran Airtour, managed to lease – besides Ukrainian MD 82s – Boeing 737-300 equipment from Jordan Aviation.

Although Iran Air had only received a very limited number of new aircraft, compared to its needs, the delivery of the new equipment had an impact on the balance sheet of the carrier. For the first time in years, the national flag carrier posted an operating profit of 410bn rials (£2.87m) in Fiscal Year 2018–19. This was the result of improved performance in several fields, including ticket sales, technical and engineering services and more efficient use of human and other resources. With the new equipment that had arrived, Iran Air had boosted its image and attracted more domestic passengers. And as new aircraft had replaced older or obsolete planes, operating costs had decreased. Notwithstanding the operating profit, Iran Air still had a negative net profit.[9] (Net profit being the remaining income of the company after deducting all costs incurred by the company, which include expenses, taxes and interests.)

**As Iran Air was not able to buy new aircraft, it had to lease foreign aircraft like this one from Ukraine. (Iran Air)**

Just like Iran Air, Iran Airtour had to lease McDonnell Douglas MD-83 aircraft from Ukrainian carrier Bukovyna. This one is seen here landing in Tehran. (Mohammad Rozve)

To supplement its fleet, Iran Airtour had to lease this Boeing 737-300 from Jordan Aviation. (Firat Cimenti)

Iran Airtour managed to lease this Airbus A320-200 from Khors Aircompany in Ukraine. (Iran Air)

# Chapter 10
# Covid-19

The new American sanctions against Iran certainly affected Iran Air's development. The carrier, which had hoped to fully modernise its fleet, only saw the arrival of a few Western aircraft. The boycott also made maintenance more difficult and costly. Nevertheless, Iranian airlines have not suffered any grave deterioration in their safety record due to the sanctions. In fact, consistent with international trends, the number of fatalities caused by air accidents in Iran dropped.[1] Washington's decision to further boycott the Iranian aviation industry not only made it impossible for Iran to buy new aircraft or spare parts, but also hit front companies that were set up to source aircraft and parts for Iranian carriers. However, one might wonder whether the sanctions imposed by the Trump administration really hurt Iran Air… or just saved the airline from bankruptcy. Indeed, the airline had placed massive orders for new aircraft with the intention of rejuvenating its fleet and expanding its network. But just like nearly all other airlines around the world, Iran Air had to ground its fleet once the Covid pandemic spread. What if Iran Air had been able to take delivery of a larger number of ordered new planes just before the pandemic? The aircraft would have been grounded as well and it would have been nearly impossible for Iran Air to finance the purchase or lease contracts, as grounded aircraft do not generate income! So maybe one could say Iran Air survived… thanks to Trump's boycott. In the meantime, however, Joe Biden replaced Trump as president and claimed that his administration would seek a return to the multilateral deal with Tehran if the Islamic Republic would also restore its compliance with the pact. What this will mean for the future delivery of new aircraft to Iran Air and other Iranian carriers still has to be seen, as negotiations drag on.[2]

Notwithstanding the American sanctions, Iran Air outlined an ambitious network expansion plan in November 2019. With the new ATR equipment, the airline had been able to consider regional and domestic expansion. A number of new domestic routes were launched, some of which are still active, while others had been of a rather experimental nature. About half of the ten new domestic routes from the new hub in Bandar Abbas are still active. Flights between Tehran and Gorgan, Nowshar, Dezful, Ramsar, Rasht, Ahvaz, Shiraz and Qeshm Island are also still active. Other routes to mainly smaller and newly opened airports such as Kalaleh, Jask, Kashan and Iranshahr were only short-lived.[3] Furthermore, ATRs were introduced on international routes, like the twice-weekly service between Tabriz and Baku (Azerbaijan). The aircraft were also used on charter operations from Kermanshah to Najaf in Iraq for the Arbaeen season. (The Arbaeen is one of the most important ceremonies in the Shi'ite Muslim calendar.) One has to keep in mind, however, that many regional routes in Iran are not profitable. Such services are motivated by non-commercial factors for the airline, such as boosting the regional connectivity of remote areas in terms of air traffic.

Iran Air seldom operated flights at full capacity. Nevertheless, when the Covid-19 pandemic hit, the airline slashed its passenger capacity further to ensure social distancing. Ticket sales for ATR planes were reduced from 65 seats to 45, those for Airbus aircraft from 130 to 100, and the capacity on Fokker planes was reduced from 100 to 70 passengers.[4]

By early 2020, Iran Air's operations could be partly resumed after a standstill due to the Covid-19 pandemic. All scheduled flights to Europe were operated again as before, with the exception of flights to Vienna, Stockholm and Gothenburg as Austria and Sweden continued to ban Iranian flights because of the pandemic. However, Iran Air's A300/310 and 330 planes remained banned from European airspace, as these planes had not undergone software upgrades while being grounded. Also, flights from Iran to the Middle East and Asia remained grounded as several countries still kept their borders closed to contain the spread of the coronavirus.[5]

Although it is very difficult to obtain statistics regarding the activities of Iranian carriers, some figures were published anyhow. In February 2020, Iran Air had transported 265,000 passengers on 3,136 international and domestic scheduled flights, registering a more than 32 per cent growth compared with the same month of 2019. With 377,000 seats offered, the load factor reached 67 per cent (compared to 273,000 seats offered, and a load factor of 66 per cent in February 2019). Also in February 2020, the carrier transported 140 tonnes of postal shipments.[6] With the reintroduction of international services, figures further increased. By June 2020, the airline transported 10,817 passengers on such international services, a 60 per cent hike compared with the same month a year earlier.[7] In October 2020, after Austria opened its borders again, Iran Air could resume a weekly flight to Vienna, followed by a weekly flight to Ankara in December. Despite the pandemic that had largely disrupted mainly international air travel, Iran Air also launched two new services to Europe. Due to the general outlook of the aviation sector and the limited fleet of the carrier, such a move was rather remarkable. The opening of a Tehran–Madrid service was planned for 2 September 2020 and the weekly flight would be operated by Airbus A330 equipment. Later, an – also weekly – route to Manchester would be opened.

Whereas Iran Air had received a few new aircraft, the carrier also had to consider removing the oldest aircraft from its fleet. Therefore, in September 2020, a total of 11 old aircraft was put up for auction. These included several Boeing 747s. At the last minute, a 12th aircraft, which had also been put up for sale, was donated to the aviation museum at the Tehran Aviation Exhibition.[8]

**Just like other airlines worldwide, Iran Air had to follow strict Covid-19 regulations, including disinfecting the aircraft. (Iran Air)**

Due to the COVID-19 pandemic, this Airbus A320 – obtained in 2009 from Vertir Airlines in Armenia – had to be stored in 2020. (Iran Air)

With the new ATR equipment, the airline could consider opening up new regional and domestic routes. (Chrisrabinson, CC BY-SA 4.0, https://creativecommons.org/licenses/by-sa/4.0, via Wikimedia Commons)

# Chapter 11
# The Outlook for Iran Air

Predicting the future of an airline is an impossible task. Airlines are so much more than companies that fly passengers and cargo from one point to another. They are influenced by a large number of factors, like economic upturns or depressions, geopolitical factors and the spread of pandemics, and sometimes they are even part of the policy of their governments. Nobody could have predicted that airline operations would have come to a near complete standstill due to the Covid-19 pandemic. Nor would it have been possible to predict the impact of the Russian–Ukrainian war on the airline industry. If airlines around the world feel this impact, it is even more harmful to airlines that have to operate under difficult circumstances resulting from an international boycott and domestic politics. Therefore, the outlook for Iran Air remains in the dark. But the fact the airline managed to survive for many years under these difficult circumstances underlines the capabilities of its management and the will to withstand the challenges of its specific operating environment.

When the Covid-19 pandemic was still limiting international travel, Iran Air launched several routes. In some cases, older services, which had been suspended, were revived. In other cases, new destinations were added to the route map. In April 2021, it was announced the carrier would start operating twice-weekly flights between Tehran and London Heathrow. This service had been suspended earlier during a new coronavirus variant outbreak in the UK in December 2020.[1] Following a decision by the Iranian Health Ministry, flights to Paris were resumed in June 2021, with services to Pakistan starting back up a few days later.[2] The gradual return to the original flight schedules had its impact on the performance of the airline. In June 2021, Iran Air transported 130,525 passengers via 2,389 flights. Passenger numbers on international flights particularly increased. No fewer than 36,516 people were transported via 305 international flights that month, as demand for air travel was recovering amid accelerated vaccination campaigns against the virus. That is a 115 per cent growth compared to the previous month. The total revenue-generating flight hours in that month stood at 3,984 hours of which 2,966 hours (or 74 per cent) belonged to domestic flights and the rest to international flights. With 222,863 seats offered, the load factor stood at 58 per cent, which is nearly the maximum allowed occupancy rate considering National Coronavirus Headquarters' instructions, which restricted maximum capacity to 60 per cent.[3, 4] Using its ATR fleet, Iran Air could also start up the Bandar Abbas–Dubai flight as of November 2021. In January 2022, another regional service between Mashhad International Airport in the capital of the Khorasan Razavi Province and Lahore in Pakistan was initiated.[5] As of April 2022, Iran Air returned to Kuwait as well. Kuwait Airport is one of Iran Air's oldest flight destinations in the Middle East. On 7 April 2022, a direct flight from Shiraz International Airport to Kuwait was resumed with a stop in Isfahan on the return leg. A second Shiraz-Isfahan-Kuwait-Shiraz flight route followed on 20 April. As a result, Iran Air operated flights from Abadan, Ahvaz, Lar, Mashhad and Isfahan to Kuwait International Airport.[6]

Considering the evolution of the Covid-19 pandemic and the resulting increase in demand for air travel, it is understandable that Iran Air once again tried to rejuvenate its fleet. The fact that the Donald Trump administration had made room for Joe Biden was another factor that inspired Iran Air to try to press Boeing to revive the carrier's order, signed in 2016. Road and Urban Development

Minister Mohammad Eslami even went a step further and stated Boeing should be held accountable for the delay in carrying out its contract with Iran Air. In his interview with Forbes.com,[7] he went on to say that, 'Iranian companies have the right as per the contract to pursue their contract'. It was clear the ongoing negotiations about a new nuclear deal might just offer new hope that Iran Air would be removed from a boycott list. At the same time, Iran Air also tried to obtain spare parts for its ATR fleet, of which seven were still active in March 2022, whereas the other aircraft were grounded in anticipation of required maintenance.[8]

When I was finishing the last pages of this book in May 2022, the Biden administration still believed the 2015 nuclear agreement was worth restoring as a means of ensuring that Iran does not acquire a nuclear weapon.[9] In exchange, the United States would lift its export restrictions regarding aircraft and aircraft parts. Unfortunately, President Biden and his administration are distracted because of the sudden Russian invasion of Ukraine and the subsequent war, which receives full attention. Furthermore, the president's position at home may be weakened in advance of the mid-term elections. The Democrats are very worried that 2024 could bring Donald Trump back into the White House. In such a case, a new nuclear deal would only last some two years; as in the past, the lifting of boycott measures only lasted long enough to enable the delivery of a few Airbus and ATR aircraft. Therefore, Iran Air's chance to obtain more essential new aircraft will likely depend not only on the willingness of the Iranian leaders to agree upon acceptable terms for a new nuclear deal, but also on the outcome of the American presidential elections in 2024. However, Iran Air has survived more than four decades of boycotts, so it is highly probable the carrier will also survive this further delay.

While it is clear that Iran Air's future will mainly depend on the outcome of further talks between the American and Iranian governments regarding a new nuclear deal, the flag carrier also has to face some domestic competition. Besides Iran Aseman Airlines (which was mentioned earlier in this book), one of the main competitors could be Mahan Airlines, which operates under the name Mahan Air. This privately owned carrier was established in 1991 and started operations in June 1992. The Mahan Air fleet has gone through an extensive modernisation since 2006 as Boeing 747-400s, Airbus A300-600s, Avro RJ-100s and Airbus A340-600s were gradually acquired. By 2015, the airline carried 5.4 million passengers per year. Based on fleet size and seat numbers, Mahan Air is the largest Iranian airline, with destinations in Europe, the Far East and the Middle East. Furthermore, the airline has an extensive domestic network.[10] In Asia, China is the carrier's main destination with flights to Shanghai, Guangzhou and Beijing. In Europe, the airline started up operations to Milan, Athens, Barcelona and Paris. But in 2020, the carrier lost its traffic rights to Spain after a French ban had already resulted in the cancellation of the four-weekly service to Paris. And during the Covid-19 pandemic, the carrier had to also cancel its flights to China, although it operated a few flights to evacuate Iranian citizens. In May 2022, the carrier offered international flights to Ankara, Baghdad, Bangkok, Delhi, Dubai, Guangzhou, Lahore and Moscow on its website. Caspian Airlines is another international carrier that operates – besides domestic flights –routes to destinations in the Middle East. Although its current status is not clear, it seems the carrier mainly operates leased McDonnel Douglas aircraft of the MD-model range. Kish Air – with its main base at the popular Kish Island – might be another competitor for Iran Air. The airline is a joint venture between Kish Free Zone Organization, Kish Investment and Development, plus Kish Development and Servicing. It was established in 1989 and started operations in 1990. Just like Caspian, the carrier mainly operates international flights to destinations in the Middle East, as well as domestic flights. Although the carrier had to begin its operations with older aircraft, in recent years, two Airbus A321-200s were added to the fleet. Qeshm Air was founded in 1993 and started out operations with leased aircraft, at first on the Qeshm–Tehran domestic route, followed by flights to Dubai. Currently, the carrier operates a network of domestic routes with a fleet including Airbus A319, A320 and A321 aircraft.

Taban Airlines, trading under the name of Taban Air, was established in 2005 by Captain Asghar Abdollahpour and has its base in Tehran. The carrier offers domestic and international destinations with a fleet that includes Boeing 737-400s and -500s, alongside some McDonnell Douglas MD-88s. As Taban Air also operates charter flights, it can be considered a competitor of Iran Airtour, rather than Iran Air. The name 'Karun Airlines' may sound new, but the airline was already established in 1992 as Iranian Naft Airlines. It is owned and operated by the Retirement Organization of the National Iranian Oil Company. In September 2017, the airline was renamed Karun Airlines. It offers cargo and passenger scheduled and charter services within Iran and to neighbouring regions, but given its limited size, it should not be considered as a serious competitor of Iran Air.[11] Zagros Airlines was founded in 2005 in Abadan and uses both the Abadan and Tehran airports as operating bases. In 2007, the carrier started its first international route to Damascus.[12] In September 2013, the airline obtained its Airbus A320-200, followed by an A319 in 2016, and in 2017 the carrier added an Airbus A321-200 to its fleet, on wet lease from Khors Aircompany in Ukraine. In July 2019, Zagros Airlines became the first Iranian airliner to employ a female pilot since the Iranian Revolution. For the moment, the airline only lists Baghdad and Najaf in Iraq as international destinations on its website.[13] ATA Airlines was established in 2008 but had to wait until 2010 to start up domestic operations. Once again, domestic destinations form the core of its operations. The airline has a fleet, composed of Airbus A320s and Boeing 737s.

Sepehran Airlines is one of the newer entrants to the market. The airline operates from Mashhad International Airport with secondary bases in Shiraz and Tehran. In April 2015, the carrier obtained its first aircraft, a Boeing 737-500. By 2021, the fleet had grown to include a total of six 737s of different types, as well as a single Dornier 328JET. Fly Persia also recently entered the market. In 2019, the carrier operated its first flight from Shiraz to Mashhad. It currently only serves domestic destinations, with a fleet of three Boeing 737s.

Merah Airlines is perhaps Iran Air's most aggressive new competitor. The airline operates a series of domestic routes but also has a strong presence in the international market. Furthermore, the carrier managed to modernise its fleet, which includes Airbus A319s, A321s, A340-300s and Embraer ERJ 145ERs. Finally, it needs to be mentioned that the government is planning on reviving Pars Air under the registered name of Pars Ocean Kish Company. The airline would operate a fleet of Canadian-made CRJ-200s.

It is clear Iran Air has to face competition from many Iranian carriers, some of which have a long history and others of which were established in more recent years. However, most of these airlines are rather small – with the exception of Mahan Air – and do not have the potential of seriously competing with the flag carrier. Furthermore, these competitors face the same problems as Iran Air itself when it comes to maintenance, purchasing of spare parts and aircraft, plus hiring qualified staff. Therefore, one could say they are all operating on a level playing field. As such, they should not be considered as a major threat to the future of the flag carrier.

**Competitor Mahan Air managed to obtain modern aircraft, like this Airbus A340. (N509FZ, CC BY-SA 4.0 https://creativecommons.org/licenses/by-sa/4.0, via Wikimedia Commons)**

**Mahan Air's Boeing 747-400 seen at Dubai Airport. (Simisa, CC BY-SA 3.0 https://creativecommons.org/licenses/by-sa/3.0, via Wikimedia Commons)**

Caspian Airlines seems to mainly operate McDonnell Douglas aircraft from the MD-model range. (Javidfa, CC BY-SA 4.0 https://creativecommons.org/licenses/by-sa/4.0, via Wikimedia Commons)

A Kish Air McDonnell Douglas MD-82. (Alan Wilson from Stilton, Peterborough, Cambs, UK, CC BY-SA 2.0 https://creativecommons.org/licenses/by-sa/2.0, via Wikimedia Commons)

A Qeshm Air Airbus A300-600 seen at Istanbul Ataturk Airport. (Maor X, CC BY-SA 4.0 https://creativecommons.org/licenses/by-sa/4.0, via Wikimedia Commons)

Taban Air is a competitor for Iran Airtour, rather than for Iran Air. (Tabanairlines, CC BY-SA 4.0 https://creativecommons.org/licenses/by-sa/4.0, via Wikimedia Commons)

Taban Air also used the BAE 146 on its domestic services. (Waka77, Public domain, via Wikimedia Commons)

Karun Airlines mainly operates older aircraft like this Fokker 100. (Amin Nouabahr, CC BY-SA 4.0 https://creativecommons.org/licenses/by-sa/4.0, via Wikimedia Commons)

A Zagros Airlines Airbus A320 joined the fleet in 2013. (Mjhanpoor1, CC BY-SA 4.0 https://creativecommons.org/licenses/by-sa/4.0, via Wikimedia Commons)

An ATA Airbus A320 in a special livery. (Alec Wilson from Khon Kaen, Thailand, CC BY-SA 2.0 https://creativecommons.org/licenses/by-sa/2.0, via Wikimedia Commons)

This ATA Airbus A320 was leased in Ukraine. (Anna Zvereva from Tallinn, Estonia, CC BY-SA 2.0 https://creativecommons.org/licenses/by-sa/2.0, via Wikimedia Commons)

ATA also used Boeing 737-500s, like this one which was leased from Khors Aircompany in Ukraine. (Alec Wilson from Khon Kaen, Thailand, CC BY-SA 2.0 https://creativecommons.org/licenses/by-sa/2.0, via Wikimedia Commons)

**Sepehran Airlines is one of the new carriers in Iran. (Javidfa, CC BY-SA 4.0 https://creativecommons.org/licenses/by-sa/4.0, via Wikimedia Commons)**

**Fly Persia operates a fleet of Boeing 737s. (FlyPersia)**

**Meraj Airlines operates a modern fleet including this Airbus A321. (aeroprints.com, CC BY-SA 3.0 https://creativecommons.org/licenses/by-sa/3.0, via Wikimedia Commons)**

**A Meraj Airlines Airbus A320 at Tehran Airport. (Amin Nouabahr, CC BY-SA 4.0 https://creativecommons.org/licenses/by-sa/4.0, via Wikimedia Commons)**

Iran Air uses this Airbus A330 to compete with Mahan Air on long-haul flights. (Dara Zarbaf)

Part of the Iran Air fleet at Tehran Mehrabad Airport. (Hansueli Krapf, CC BY-SA 3.0 https://creativecommons.org/licenses/by-sa/3.0, via Wikimedia Commons)

# Appendix 1
# Incidents and Accidents

(Based on information from the Accident Safety Network)

## Iran Air

Before Iranian Airways and PAS merged to form Iran Air in 1962, they both had several accidents. Iranian Airways lost six Douglas DC-3s in crashes and a fire between 1949 and 1959. One of its Douglas DC-4s was shot down. Persian Air Services lost three Avro Yorks in crashes and a maintenance accident between 1955 and 1959.[1] These accidents are not discussed in this appendix as they do not relate to Iran Air itself. Furthermore, Iran Air experienced several other incidents, mostly hijackings, of which no details are available.

On 14 September 1955, an Iranian Airways Douglas DC-3 (EP-AAG), bound for Saudi Arabia, crashed shortly after taking off from Tehran Mehrabad International Airport. The nine people on board the aircraft – all airline employees – were killed.

On 25 December 1952, an Iranian Airways Douglas DC-3 with 21 passengers and a crew of four on board crashed while approaching Tehran Airport. There was one survivor.

On 2 January 1962, a C-47D (EP-ABB) crashed at Kabul International Airport. Flight IR 123 was a scheduled international cargo flight from Kabul to Tehran. The co-pilot was in the left-hand seat and in control of the aircraft at the commencement of the take-off run. When accelerating for take-off, the pilot-in-command noticed the propeller of the number 1 engine was over-speeding and surging as high as 3,000rpm. As the aircraft approached an indicated an airspeed of about 80kts, the captain took command. He noticed the aircraft was headed to the left, away from the runway centreline, towards three runway lights in a concrete footing at the left edge of the runway. To avoid a possible collision with the lights, the captain applied elevator control and lifted the aircraft off the runway. The over-speeding propeller condition did not subside, although the crew followed the procedure prescribed in the operations manual for corrective action. The flight path was about 30 to 45° to the left of the runway and in the general direction of the Kabul Airport terminal building. Therefore, the captain attempted to turn the aircraft further to the left to avoid collision with the building. About 325ft from the south edge of Runway 29, the left wing made contact with the ground and the aircraft crashed. Nobody was killed, but the aircraft was damaged beyond repair.

On 20 February 1962, a Douglas C-47A (EP-AEI) was damaged beyond repair near the Ahwaz Airport in Iran. No further details are known.

On 4 May 1964, a Douglas R4D (DC-3) (EP-ADI) was damaged beyond repair in Isfahan (Iran). No further details are known.

On 15 February 1965, a Vickers 782D Viscount (EP-AHC) was damaged beyond repair at Isfahan Shahid Beheshti Airport. The Viscount landed heavily, causing the left main gear to collapse. The aircraft veered off the side of the runway. There were no casualties.

On 17 March 1967, a Douglas C-47A (DC-3) (EP-AEF) was damaged beyond repair at Bandar Abbas Airport in Iran. The aircraft struck a dirt mount on landing, forcing the pilot to carry out an overshoot. The aircraft circled the airport to burn up fuel and then made a wheels-up landing. There were no casualties.

On 21 June 1970, a Boeing 727 (registration unknown) was hijacked on a domestic scheduled passenger flight from Tehran Mehrabad Airport to Abadan Airport. The hijacking lasted less than one day. There were no casualties.

On 10 October 1970, a Boeing 727 (registration unknown) was hijacked by three hijackers who demanded to be taken to Iraq where they threatened to blow up the plane unless Iran would release 21 political prisoners. The three hijackers eventually surrendered. There were no casualties.

On 21 January 1980, a Boeing 727 (EP-IRD) crashed during a snowstorm on approach to Tehran Mehrabad Airport. The aircraft had departed from Mashhad Airport. All 120 passengers and eight crew members were killed. The aircraft had been cleared for an ILS approach to Runway 29 but crashed in the Elburz Mountain Range north of Tehran. The investigation revealed the pilot did not follow the ATS route but proceeded straight to Mehrabad Airport. About six minutes before impact, air traffic control (ATC) asked the pilot to make a 360° turn over the Varamin Non-Directional Beacon (NDB). The pilot made this to the north without advising ATC. On approach, the co-pilot pointed out the VORTAC radial was crossing on the wrong track, but the pilot did not react. An inoperable ILS and ground radar were considered as probable causes of the accident.

On 7 January 1983, a Boeing 727 (EP-IRA) was damaged beyond repair at Tehran Mehrabad Airport. Control over the aircraft was lost during a high-speed taxi check. The aircraft ran off the side of the runway, causing severe damage to the undercarriage and the fuselage. The taxi check was performed by two mechanics instead of by a qualified crew member.

On 6 July 1983, a Boeing 747 on its way from Shiraz Airport to Tehran Mehrabad Airport was hijacked by six Iranian males armed with pistols, sub-machine guns and explosives. The hijackers did not make any immediate demands but allowed the aircraft to land at Kuwait Airport to refuel and obtain food and water. While on the ground, they also released 186 of the 390 passengers. After departure from Kuwait, the hijackers demanded to be flown to Baghdad in Iraq, but the crew convinced them to proceed to Paris. After landing, the hijackers demanded, and were allowed, to talk to the leader of the Paris-based People's Mujahideen guerrilla movement. The man convinced the hijackers to surrender. The remaining passengers and crew were then released unharmed. The hijackers were sentenced to three years in prison for air piracy.

On 26 June 1984, a Boeing 727 (registration unknown) performed a domestic passenger flight from Tehran Mehrabad Airport to Bushehr Airport. Two men hijacked the plane and forced the pilot to fly to Qatar where the aircraft was refuelled and the 125 passengers were released. The aircraft then proceeded to Cairo where it was granted permission to land as it was dangerously low on fuel. After an overnight stay, the hijackers forced the pilot to fly to Baghdad, where they surrendered and requested political asylum.

On 7 August 1984, an Airbus A300 (registration unknown) performed a scheduled passenger flight from Tehran Mehrabad Airport to Jeddah Airport. Two hijackers, armed with a knife and a fake bomb, hijacked the aircraft carrying 304 passengers and 11 crew members. The aircraft was diverted after a stop in Shiraz.

The aircraft then flew on to Bahrain for refuelling and to Cairo before landing in Rome. The hijackers had demanded to go to Paris and request political asylum, but the aircraft was not allowed to enter French airspace. Then, as these demands were not met, the hijackers surrendered to officials in Rome.

On 28 August 1984, a domestic scheduled passenger flight operated by Airbus A300 (EP-IBS) was hijacked by two young men and a woman, claiming to have explosives. They diverted the aircraft to Baghdad. The hijackers' original destination was Kuwait, but airport authorities denied the aircraft permission to land. Upon landing in Baghdad, the hijackers requested political asylum. The aircraft was impounded and returned to Iran following the Gulf War in September 1990.

On 9 September 1984, a Boeing 727 (registration unknown) was hijacked by a police officer and a family of four while performing a scheduled passenger flight from Bandar Abbas Airport to Tehran Mehrabad Airport. The aircraft initially flew to Abu Dhabi but was refused permission to land. After refuelling stops in Bahrain and Cairo, where 52 passengers escaped, the aircraft landed at an airfield near Basra in Iraq. The hijackers were armed with a grenade, pistol and knife. The hijackers released the remaining crew and passengers in exchange for promised asylum.

On 12 September 1984, an Airbus A300 (registration unknown) on a domestic scheduled flight from Tehran Mehrabad Airport to Shiraz Airport was hijacked by four people. Security guards, positioned aboard the aircraft, thwarted the attempt. Two of the hijackers were wounded in the takeover attempt. Upon landing at Isfahan Airport in Iran, the hijackers were taken into custody. Upon questioning, the hijackers confessed to having been supporters of the outlawed Mujahedin Khalq, an underground group that opposed Khomeini's regime.

On 5 August 1985, two people attempted to hijack an Iran Air Boeing 727 (registration unknown) on a domestic flight from Tehran Mehrabad Airport to Bandar Abbas Airport. The in-flight security guards of the Islamic Revolutionary Guards Corps shot and killed one hijacker and arrested the other. The aircraft landed safely at Bandar Abbas Airport without further incident.

On 2 November 1985, an attempt to hijack an Iran Air Boeing 707 (registration unknown) on a domestic flight from Bandar Abbas to Tehran was thwarted by in-flight guards of the Revolutionary Guards Corps. The hijacker, acting alone, tried to enter the cockpit of the aircraft with a package and reportedly threatened to blow up the plane before being overpowered by the in-flight guards. There were no reported injuries. The demands of the hijacker are unknown. It is believed, however, that the attempted hijacking was an effort to overshadow the anniversary of the seizure of the American Embassy in Tehran on 1 November 1979.

On 15 October 1986, a Boeing 737-200 (EP-IRG) was damaged beyond repair when Iraqi aircraft attacked the Shiraz airport. Passengers were deplaning at the time of the attack. Three passengers were killed. According to Iranian authorities, a number of C-130 Hercules aircraft, parked at the airport, were also destroyed.

On 10 November 1986, an Iran Air Airbus A300 (registration unknown) was on a scheduled domestic flight from Tehran to Tabriz when an armed man and woman attempted to hijack the aircraft. The pair were reportedly thwarted in the attempt by security officers and the aircraft continued to its scheduled destination. There were no reported injuries.

On 3 July 1988, Iran Air Flight 451 – on an international scheduled passenger flight from Tehran via Bandar Abbas Airport to Dubai – arrived at Bandar Abbas from Tehran at 0840hrs. The Airbus A300 (EP-IBU) was to continue to Dubai as flight 655. Prior to departure, the crew received an en-route clearance to Dubai via the planned route along airways A59 and A59W at FL140. The plane took off from Runway 21 at 1017hrs and climbed straight ahead. Two minutes later, the crew reported leaving 3,500ft for FL140 on airway A59. At 1024hrs, the Airbus was hit by surface-to-air missiles. The tail and one wing broke off as a result of the explosions. Control was lost and the aircraft crashed in the sea. All 274 passengers and 16 crew members perished. The missiles were fired by the US Navy cruiser USS *Vincennes*, operating in the area with the frigates USS *Elmer Montgomery* and USS *John H Sides*. They were to protect other ships in the area. At about the time the Airbus took off, the radar aboard USS *Vincennes* picked up a brief Identification Friend or Foe (IFF) Mode 2 response, which led to the mistaken identification of the Airbus as a hostile F-14 aircraft. The USS *Vincennes* issued seven challenges on the Military Air Distress (MAD) frequency 243Mhz, addressed to 'Iranian Aircraft', 'Iranian Fighter' or 'Iranian F-14'. These messages were followed by three challenges on the International Air Defence (IAD) radio frequency (121.5Mhz). Due to increasing tension in the area – on 17 May 1987, an Iraqi Mirage had attacked USS *Stark* – all aircraft in the area had to monitor 121.5Mhz. But Iran Air did not respond to the messages of USS *Vincennes*. Meanwhile, radar operators were monitoring the Aegis screens. They reported that the incoming plane was descending with an increasing speed. But, in fact, the Airbus was climbing. Considering itself and USS *Elmer Montgomery* under aggression, USS *Vincennes* took the ultimate decision to launch missiles against the perceived hostile target. It remains uncertain whether the Iran Air flight crew (only able to monitor the IAD and not the MAD frequencies) would have been able to rapidly identify their flight as the subject of the challenges made by the USS *Vincennes*.

On 22 October 1988, a Boeing 747 (registration unknown) executed a flight from Tehran to Vienna and Frankfurt as IR 723. The aircraft was hijacked by two passengers, armed with a knife and a handgun. The hijacking occurred about half an hour before the plane was due to land in Vienna. The flight crew then reported to the Vienna ATC that they were diverting to London because of (unconfirmed) bad weather at Vienna and Frankfurt. Meanwhile, security guards came down from the upper deck and overpowered the hijackers. The flight continued to Frankfurt after 45 minutes on the ground in London.

On 26 January 1990, an attempt was made to hijack an Iran Air Boeing 727 (registration unknown) on a domestic scheduled passenger flight from Shiraz Airport to Bandar Abbas Airport. Four passengers, carrying pistols and hand grenades, demanded the flight be diverted to either Iraq or Israel. However, Iranian security forces aboard the flight killed the hijackers. No passengers were injured and the flight safely returned to Shiraz.

On 9 June 1996, a Boeing 727 (EP-IRU) was destroyed while operating a training flight. The aircraft took off from Tehran Mehrabad Airport on a flight to Rasht Airport. After the 15th touch-and-go, the aircraft landed on Runway 09 with the undercarriage retracted and slid about 2,100m (2,200 yards) before it became airborne again. A fire developed in the rear fuselage as the aircraft circled the airport. The undercarriage was deployed manually, and the flight was cleared to land for Runway 09. However, the fire affected the aircraft systems and the pilot experienced control difficulties. The left wing made contact with the ground, after which the aircraft impacted in a rice field. The aircraft broke up, killing four of the seven crew members.

On 6 October 1997, Iran Air flight 257 was hijacked while en route from Tehran to Bandar Abbas. The flight was operated by Boeing 727 (registration unknown). A passenger, armed with a handgun, burst into the cockpit. He demanded to be flown to Iraq but reportedly also mentioned Israel as a secondary destination. At some point, the hijacker fired a shot and wounded a security guard. Another security guard opened fire, wounded the hijacker and placed him under arrest. The plane continued onto Badar Abbas, where the hijacker was taken into custody.

On 5 January 1998, Iran Air flight 378, flown by a Fokker 100 (EP-IDC) departed Urmia (Orymiyeh) on a scheduled domestic flight to Tehran Mehrabad Airport. The flight was descending towards Tehran when the crew decided to divert to Isfahan. Weather conditions at Tehran were not suitable for a landing on Runway 29, as visibility was poor in snow and sleet, and there was a 20kts tailwind. The flight positioned for an approach to Runway 26 at Isfahan. There was fog in the area and the aeroplane descended until it crashed in a dry riverbed short of the runway. The badly damaged aircraft was stored at Isfahan for a while and then sold to Flight West Airlines in Australia for spares. Nobody was injured.

On 2 February 2000, the crew of a Lockheed C-130 Hercules transport plane operated by the Iranian Air Force lost directional control during take-off from Runway 29R at Tehran Mehrabad Airport. The aircraft collided with an Iran Air Airbus A300 (EP-IBR), which was being towed to a hangar. Both aircraft were destroyed by fire. There were eight casualties on the ground.

On 24 September 2000, a Fokker 100 (registration unknown) was hijacked by an armed man with a fake pistol and a gasoline bomb while on a domestic scheduled flight from Shiraz to Tehran. The lone hijacker, who demanded to be taken to France, attempted to start a fire on the aircraft but was quickly overpowered by in-flight security officers. The plane was diverted to the airport at Isfahan, where the hijacker was handed over to the authorities.

On 15 January 2004, an Iran Air Boeing 747SP (EP-IAC) suffered problems with the hydraulic system shortly after departing Beijing. The plane returned to land, during which the nose gear collapsed. The aircraft remained in Beijing for repairs, after which it was ferried back to Tehran and withdrawn from service. Some parts were stripped and the aeroplane moved to the display at the Tehran Aerospace Exhibition. In 2009, it received a full overhaul and was restored to flying condition.

On 2 January 2008, an Iran Air Fokker 100 (EP-IDB) was damaged beyond repair when it crashed on take-off from Tehran Mehrabad Airport on a domestic scheduled flight to Shiraz. Four crew members and seven passengers sustained serious injuries. The co-pilot who was Pilot Flying, performed a walk around prior to departure. Since it had been snowing, and temperatures were around freezing, he requested de-icing. Because there were a number of aircraft already waiting for de-icing, the pilot-in-command decided not to perform this procedure. When the aircraft took off, it rolled left wing down shortly after lift-off. The left wing touched the ground, after which the aircraft rolled momentarily back to a more neutral position. A few seconds later, while losing altitude, the wing touched the ground again, and when the aircraft rolled back to a more neutral attitude, both main landing gears touched the ground. All gears broke off and the aircraft slid on the area next to the runway. During the impact, all electrical power was lost. When the aircraft came to a rest, a fire developed, starting from the left-wing root towards the fuselage. All passengers and crew were evacuated through the two right-wing emergency exits.

On 19 January 2009, an Iran Air Fokker 100 (EP-CFN) landed on Runway 26L at Tehran Mehrabad Airport. Upon landing, the right-hand main landing gear broke. The aeroplane went off the right side of the runway, coming to rest between Taxiways 8 and 10. Nobody was killed.

On 18 November 2009, a Fokker 100 (EP-CFO) was substantially damaged when the left-hand main landing gear failed at Isfahan Airport while taking off for Tehran. Shortly after take-off, the undercarriage failed to retract. The crew decided to return to Isfahan. After touch-down, the shock absorber of the left main landing gear broke and the left-hand wing struck the runway. There were no casualties.

On 16 January 2010, an Iran Air Fokker 100 (registration EP-IDA) – on a flight from Tehran to Isfahan with 16 passengers on board – experienced a gear collapse when landing at Isfahan runway. The aeroplane came to a stop on the runway. No injuries occured.[2]

On 9 January 2011, a Boeing 727 (EP-IRP) originating from Tehran, crashed near its destination city of Oromiyeh, 740km (460 miles) northwest of Tehran during an attempted go-around in poor weather. It was carrying 105 people, of which at least 78 perished. The combination of bad weather and the cockpit crew's failure to deal with the situation was considered the major cause of the accident.

On 18 October 2011, a Boeing 727 (EP-IRR) operating a flight from Moscow to Mehrabad Airport landed with its nose landing gear jammed in the retracted position. Nobody was hurt.

On 19 March 2019, a Fokker 100 (EP-IDG) suffered a failure of one of the hydraulic systems. Consequently, the main undercarriage could not be lowered. Even manual attempts to deploy the undercarriage using an emergency procedure proved fruitless. The flight crew then performed a gear-up landing at Tehran Mehrabad Airport. There were no injuries. Investigation showed the aircraft had already suffered hydraulic issues on prior flights.

On 4 March 2021, a Fokker 100 (EP-CFM) operated a scheduled domestic flight from Ahwaz to Mashad Airport. According to the Revolutionary Guard, authorities disrupted the attempted hijacking of the jet. Its website stated the hijacking targeted a flight heading from Ahwaz to Mashad. The flight made an emergency landing at Isfahan Airport. Nobody was injured.

# Iran Airtour

On 8 February 1993, shortly after departure from Tehran International Airport, a Tupolev Tu-154 (Iran Airtour flight 962) crashed into a Sukhoi Su-24 fighter of the Iranian Air Force, which was landing. In this accident, all 133 people (both pilots of the Su-24 and Tupolev Tu-154, all 12 crew members and 119 passengers on board) died. The main cause was pilot error by the Su-24 pilot.

On 12 February 2002, a Tupolev Tu-154 carrying out Iran Airtour flight 956 from Tehran to Khorramabad, crashed into the Sefid Kook mountains during heavy rain, snow and dense fog. All 12 crew members and 107 passengers died.

On 1 September 2006, a Tupolev Tu-154 carrying out Iran Airtour flight 945 from Bandar Abbas to Mashad with 11 crew members and 137 passengers on board, burst into flames upon landing at Mashad airport. Of the 148 passengers and crew, 28 died.

# Appendix 2
# Iran Air Fleet Details

Considering the situation in Iran, this list might contain errors, although every effort has been made to provide correct information.

(Sources: en.wikipedia.org, Iran Air and planespotters.net)

## Historic Fleet Iran Air

| Aircraft Type | Number | First introduction | Retired | Remarks |
|---|---|---|---|---|
| Airbus A300B2 | 8 | 1978 | 2021 | |
| AirbusA300B4-200 F | 2 | 2008 | 2014 | Stored |
| Airbus A310-200 | 6 | 2001 | 2009 | |
| Airbus A320-200 | 3 | 2003 | 2004 | Leased from Nouvelair Tunisie |
| Airbus A340 | 1 | 2007 | 2007 | Leased from Conviasa |
| Avro York | ? | ? | ? | Persian Air Services prior to merger with Iranian Airways |
| Beechcraft Model 18 | ? | ? | ? | Operated by Iranian Airways prior to merger with PAS |
| Boeing 707-300 | ? | ? | 2000 | Operated by PAS prior to merger with Iranian Airways |
| Boeing 727-100 | ? | ? | 2006 | |
| Boeing 727-200 | 6 | 1974 | 2014 | Three still stored |
| Boeing 737-200 | 6 | 1971 | 2004 | Stored at Tehran Aerospace Exhibition |
| Boeing 747-100 | 6 | 1974 | 2014 | One stored |
| Boeing 747-100SF | 3 | 1983 | 1986 | Disposed of to Iran Air Force |
| Boeing 747-200B | 1 | 2007 | 2010 | |
| Boeing 747-200F | 4 | 1980 | 2004 | |
| Boeing 747-200M | 3 | 1976 | 2016 | Two stored |
| Boeing 747-400 | 1 | 2017 | 2017 | Leased from Kabo Air for Hajj flights |
| Boeing 747SP | 4 | 1976 | 2016 | Stored |
| Convair 240 | ? | ? | 1960 | |
| de Havilland Dove | ? | ? | ? | |
| de Havilland Dragon Rapide | ? | ? | ? | |
| Douglas DC-3 | ? | ? | 1972 | |
| Douglas DC-4 | ? | ? | 1960 | |

| Aircraft Type | Number | First introduction | Retired | Remarks |
|---|---|---|---|---|
| Douglas DC-6B | ? | ? | 1972 | |
| Douglas DC-7C | ? | ? | ? | |
| Douglas DC-8 | 1 | 1976 | 1977 | Leased from Martinair |
| Douglas DC-9 | 1 | 1976 | 1976 | Leased from Martinair |
| Lockheed 749 Constellation | ? | ? | ? | |
| Vickers Viscount | ? | ? | 1960 | |

## Current Fleet, Iran Air

| Airbus A300B4-200 | 1 |
|---|---|
| Airbus A300-600R | 4 |
| Airbus A310-300 | 2 |
| Airbus A319-100 | 3 |
| Airbus A320-200 | 6 |
| Airbus A321-200 | 1 |
| Airbus A330-200 | 2 |
| ATR-72-600 | 13 |
| Fokker 100 | 3 |
| McDonnell Douglas MD-82 | 2 |
| Boeing 747-200C | 1 |

## Historic Fleet, Iran Airtour

| Airbus A300-B4 | 2 |
|---|---|
| Airbus A310-300 | 1 |
| Airbus A320-200 | 2 |
| McDonnell Douglas MD 82 | 10 |
| McDonnell Douglas MD 83 | 1 |
| Tupolev Tu-154 | 17 |

## Current Fleet, Iran Airtour

| Airbus A300-600 | 4 |
|---|---|
| Airbus A310-300 | 2 |
| Airbus A320-200 | 1 |
| McDonnell Douglas MD 82 | 4 |
| McDonnell Douglas MD 83 | 1 |

# Appendix 3
# Notes and References

## Chapter 1
1. 'Iran', en.wikipedia.org.
2. Atrvash, Abbas, 'The History of Iranian Air Transportation Industry', Iran Chamber Society (online), www.iranchamber.com, January 2008.
3. 'Iran', en.wikipedia.org.
4. Ibid.
5. Atrvash, 'The History of Iranian Air Transportation Industry'.

## Chapter 2
1. Atrvash, Abbas, 'The Formation of the Iranian Air Force', Encyclopædia Iranica (online), Iranicaonline.org, 5 November 2010.
2. 'Forty Years Ago: Flight to Persia (Iran) by Walter Mittelholzer', *The Swiss Observer: The Journal of the Federation of Swiss Societies in the UK*, Heft 1451, 1964.
3. Andersson, Lennart, 'Iranian Eagles. Civil and Military Aviation in Iran 1924-1949', Andersson Aviation History Site (online), antiklar.z-bok.se.
4. Atrvash, Abbas, 'The History of Iranian Air Transportation Industry', Iran Chamber Society (online), www.iranchamber.com, January 2008.
5. Andersson, 'Iranian Eagles. Civil and Military Aviation in Iran 1924-1949'.

## Chapter 3
1. Forootan, Mostafa, 'An Analytical Study of Iran's Bilateral Air Agreements' (Master of Laws thesis), Institute of Air and Space Law, McGill University, May 1970.
2. Atrvash, Abbas, 'The History of Iranian Air Transportation Industry', Iran Chamber Society (online), www.iranchamber.com, January 2008.
3. Andersson, Lennart, 'Iranian Eagles. Civil and Military Aviation in Iran 1924-1949', Andersson Aviation History Site (online), antiklar.z-bok.se.
4. Ibid.
5. 'Iran', en.wikipedia.org.
6. Andersson, 'Iranian Eagles. Civil and Military Aviation in Iran 1924-1949'.
7. 'Iran', en.wikipedia.org.
8. Atrvash, 'The History of Iranian Air Transportation Industry'.

## Chapter 4
1. 'Iran Air', en.wikipedia.org.
2. Ibid.

## Chapter 5
1. 'Iran', en.wikipedia.org.
2. Ibid.
3. See Appendix 1: Incidents and Accidents.

4. 'Iranian Airline Development 1980-2021', www.yesterdaysairlines.com.
 5. Atrvash, Abbas, 'The History of Iranian Air Transportation Industry', Iran Chamber Society (online), www.iranchamber.com, January 2008.

# Chapter 6
 1. Forward, David, C, 'Inside Iran Air', *Airways*, November/December 1997.
 2. Ibid.
 3. 'Iran Air', en.wikipedia.org.
 4. Reuters Staff, 'Dubai airport continues to refuel Iranian planes', www.reuters.com, 5 July 2010.
 5. BBC News (online), 'Iran says its passenger jets were refused fuel abroad', www.bbc.co.uk, 5 July 2010.
 6. BBC News (online), 'Iran rejects claim that planes were denied fuel', www.bbc.co.uk, 6 July 2010
 7. 'The difficulties of Iran in Europe', Iranian Diplomacy Editorial (in Farsi), 6 August 2010.
 8. 'Iran Air flight ban in European skies', Radio Zamaneh (online), 1 June 2008.
 9. BBC News (online), 'EU imposes flight ban on Iran Air over safety', www.bbc.co.uk, 6 July 2010.
10. Karagyozova, Ralitsa, 'The sanctions on Iran's Civil Aviation', İRAM Center for Iranian Studies in Ankara (online), www.iramcenter.org, 5 May 2021.
11. Chernyavsky, Artem, 'Iran bans Russia's TU-154 planes', Pravda.ru, english.pravda.ru, 19 January 2011.
12. 'Iran to ban TU-154 flights', *The Moscow Times*, 16 January 2011.
13. EX-YU Aviation News (online), 'Iran Air to cease refuelling in EX-YU', exyuaviation.com, 24 June 2011
14. BBC News (online), 'Manston airport stops refuelling Iran Air flights', www.bbc.co.uk, 1 December 2011.

# Chapter 7
 1. 'Iran Air', en.wikipedia.org.
 2. Ibid.
 3. Ibid.
 4. CAPA Center for Aviation, 'Iran Air's fleet order signals serious intent for the Iranian Aviation industry', centreforaviation.com, 19 February 2016.
 5. Ibid.
 6. Airbus, 'Iran selects Airbus for its civil aviation renewal', airbus.com, 28 January 2016.
 7. Shantyaei, Sanam, 'France, Iran announce euro 23 billion Airbus deal', France 24.com, 28 January 2016.
 8. Reuters Staff, 'Iran orders up to 40 ATR turboprop aircraft', www.reuters.com, 1 February 2016.
 9. Reuters Staff, 'Iran Air signs contract with ATR to buy 20 planes', www.reuters.com, 10 April 2017.
10. 'Iran Air expects delayed ATR deliveries amid row with Canada', aviationiran.com, 3 September 2017.
11. Financial Tribune (online), 'No Banking hurdles for Iran Air ATR Accords', financialtribune.com, 24 May 2017.
12. '86,000 Iranians join Hajj via resumed air routes to Saudi Arabia', aviationiran.com, 25 July 2017.
13. Financial Tribune (online), '1st woman takes over as Iran Air Chief', financialtribune.com, 16 July 2017.
14. Financial Tribune (online), 'Iran Air to launch regional airline with new ATRs', financialtribune.com, 10 October 2017.

## Chapter 8

1. Aboudi, Sami and Hepher, Tim, 'Iran seals $17 billion Boeing deal, close to Airbus order'. www.reuters.com, 11 December 2016.
2. Financial Tribune (online), 'Iran unveils Boeing deal financing process', financialtribune.com, 13 December 2016.
3. Jahn, Thomas and Koenen, Jens, 'Fear and Loathing at Airbus', *Handelsblatt Today*, 29 May 2017.
4. Financial Tribune (online), 'Iran's massive plane order: a win-win for all', financialtribune.com, 19 April 2017.
5. Financial Tribune (online), 'Why Iran Air turned down Boeing's offer for two 747-8s', financialtribune.com, 4 August 2017.
6. Financial Tribune (online), 'Iran Air confirms cancellation of early Boeing delivery', financialtribune.com, 25 April 2017.
7. Financial Tribune (online), 'CAPA: Iran's decision to drop A380 Logical', financialtribune.com, 30 December 2016.
8. Hepher, Tim, 'Iran jetliner deal could take longer to complete, Airbus says', www.reuters.com, 15 January 2018.
9. Ibid.
10. Gates, Dominic, 'Boeing's $9.5 billion Iran deals, always uncertain, are now effectively dead', *The Seattle Times*, 8 May 2018.
11. Ibid.
12. Duclos, François, 'Pas de nouveaux Boeing, Airbus et ATR pour l'Iran', *Air Journal*, 9 May 2018.

## Chapter 9

1. Dudley, Dominic, 'How Iran is transforming its aviation industry with multi-billion dollar orders for hundreds of jets', forbes.com, 28 June 2017.
2. Financial Tribune (online), 'Iran Air banks on new planes to prosper', financialtribune.com, 22 May 2017.
3. Ibid.
4. Financial Tribune (online), 'Senior Official: No Sukhoi for Iran Air', financialtribune.com, 23 July 2018.
5. Financial Tribune (online), 'Gov't to issue bonds to pay back loans on Iran Air ATR planes', financialtribune.com, 24 September 2018.
6. Financial Tribune (online), 'EU urged to press US on Airbus Deliveries', financialtribune.com, 18 December 2018.
7. Financial Tribune (online), '3 secondhand Airbus jets join Iran Air Fleet', financialtribune.com, 24 February 2019.
8. Financial Tribune (online), 'Fokker 100 to rejoin Iran Air fleet after getting flight permit', financialtribune.com, 22 May 2019.
9. Financial Tribune (online), 'Iran Air posts 1st profit in years', financialtribune.com, 8 October 2019.

## Chapter 10

1. Nadimi, Farzim, 'How sanctions are affecting Iran's airline industry', The Washington Institute for Near East Policy, 17 April 2019.
2. MEE Staff, 'Joe Biden reaffirms he will seek return to Iran nuclear deal', middleeasteye.net, 2 December 2020.

3. 'Iran Air outlines network expansion plans', aviationiran.com, 6 November 2019.
4. Financial Tribune (online), 'Iran Air slashing plane capacity to ensure social distancing', financialtribune.com, 14 July 2020.
5. Financial Tribune (online), 'Iran Air resumes Europa flights', financialtribune.com, 11 March 2020.
6. Financial Tribune (online), '32% growth in Iranair passenger transport in February', financialtribune.com, 13 May 2020.
7. Financial Tribune (online), 'Iran Air's int'l flights increasing', financialtribune.com, 19 September 2020.
8. Financial Tribune (online), 'IranAir auctions off 11 aging aircraft', financialtribune.com, 16 September 2020.

# Chapter 11
1. Financial Tribune (online), 'Flights between Iran and the UK will resume on May 6', financialtribune.com, 13 April 2021.
2. Financial Tribune (online), 'IranAir is scheduled to operate flights to France and Pakistan', financialtribune.com, 20 June 2021.
3. Financial Tribune (online), 'A total of 130,525 passengers were transported by Iran's flag carrier', financialtribune.com, 31 August 2021.
4. Press TV (online), 'Iran Air reports 115 per cent surge in international passenger numbers', presstv.ir, 30 August 2021.
5. Financial Tribune (online), 'IranAir Launches Two Flights From Mashhad to Pakistan' financialtribune.com, 4 January 2022.
6. Financial Tribune (online), 'Iran's flag carrier airline will increase the number of flights from Isfahan and Shiraz to Kuwait International Airport', financialtribune.com, 17 April 2022.
7. Dudley, Dominic, 'Iran Tries to Revive $16 billion deal for 80 Boeing jets', forbes.com, 20 April 2021.
8. ch-aviation, 'Iran Air talks in tandem with nuclear talks', www.ch.aviation.com, 18 March 2022.
9. Kenyon, Peter, 'The status of Iran nuclear deal talks', news.wjet.org, 5 May 2022.
10. 'Mahan Air', en.wikipedia.org.
11. 'Karun Airlines', en.wikipedia.org.
12. 'Zagros Airlines', en.wikipedia.org.
13. Ibid.

# Appendix 1
1. 'Iran Air', en.wikipedia.org.
2. Hradecky, Simon, 'Accident: Iran Air F100 at Isfahan on Jan 15th, 2010, nose gear collapsed on landing', avherald.com, 16 January 2010.

# Other books you might like:

Airlines Series, Vol. 1

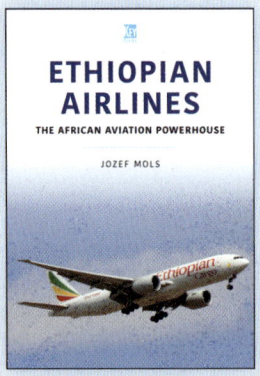
Airlines Series, Vol. 2

Airlines Series, Vol. 4

Airlines Series, Vol. 5

Airlines Series, Vol. 6

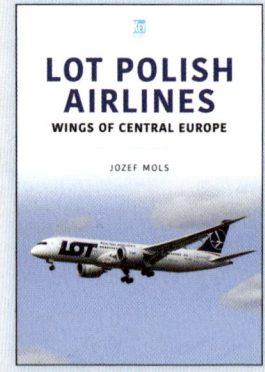
Airlines Series, Vol. 7

For our full range of titles please visit:
**shop.keypublishing.com/books**

---

# VIP Book Club

## Sign up today and receive
## TWO FREE E-BOOKS

Be the first to find out about our forthcoming book releases and receive exclusive offers.

Register now at **keypublishing.com/vip-book-club**

Our VIP Book Club is a 100% spam-free zone, and we will never share your email with anyone else. You can read our full privacy policy at: privacy.keypublishing.com